The Big Secret

A Parent's Treasure

JAMES W. MARKHAM III

ARPress
ILLUMINATING IDEAS
EMPOWERING VOICES

ARPress
45 Dan Road Suite 5
Canton MA 02021

Hotline: 1(888) 821-0229
Fax: 1(508) 545-7580

Ordering Information:

Quantity sales. Special discounts are available on quantity purchases by corporations, associations, and others. For details, contact the publisher at the address above.

Printed in the United States of America.

ISBN-13:   Softcover   979-8-89389-597-1
              eBook   979-8-89389-598-8
Library of Congress Control Number: 2024921153

Introduction

As a youngster, I learned a lot not only from my parents but also from others, especially from my grandparents and my aunt. They taught me to think, evaluate, set goals, and, most importantly, achieve them. My goal here is to teach those who have a deep desire to set goals just as I did.

I made the decision to achieve as much as I possibly could, and I continued to do just that today. I knew my plan worked. I lived it. You too can do the same if you choose to do it. Make the decision to make your life better by the self-satisfaction of making the most of everything that you have and want.

A survey from people who did not have much time to live was taken. The number one thing they all said with regret was that they wished they had tried to conquer the things they feared the most. They wished they had made an effort to scale that hurdle.

A heartfelt thanks to my fantastic relatives who taught me and my siblings the basic principle rules of life.

Do your Home Work: Get a second opinion: Do your research: Compare your options: Do you have a plan?

Denomination

The presence of many different denominations and sects in the society means that the culture is differentiated into many parts with differing group interests and viewpoints.

The world we live in has many different countries. In each of these countries, you have many different races of people. Each race of people has their own culture. In their culture, they have their own religion. In each religion, they have their own God. This is viewed **EQUALLY**.

Opinion

There were extraordinary events that happen in people's lives. There were a lot of people who had not experienced such events in their lifetime; therefore, they figure. Since these events did not happen during their lifetime, then it was not possible to happen to anyone else.

There was a movie about an airline pilot. By the events that took place, he and the others saved 155 lives. This movie was based on a true story. We all watched it on the news on TV during our lifetime.

I question your opinion. There were 155 passengers. How many people were from different countries? So how many different denominations? If all of them prayed for safety and protection, who did they pray to?

The good Lord above will sometimes put us in a dangerous situation. We survive the situation. Did this happen for a preparation for a larger future event that will happen? Knowing you handled the first event very well, then you can handle the second event better. The captain of the airplane—how many times did his God help him in saving 155 lives? One to five times? How many times did he use logic—logical common sense? Were there times when emotion was starting to take over?

Do your Home Work: Get a second opinion: Do your research: Compare your options: Do you have a plan?

Deteriorating Infrastructure

As we look at history events, there are records where one country will deteriorate the infrastructure of a different country so they can conquer and take over that country. Remember the Trojan horse and the city of Troy and how the city was conquered? That's right, from the inside out.

During our lifetime, there is a great leader of a super country who wrote a book about how to take over a mother super country without firing a shot.

Over the years, the guidelines of THAT book has penetrated and have been applied to the country that is to be taken or conquered. This is accomplished by possibly many types of influence to the people who are assigned to run the country.

There are people who have talk shows. They have guest speakers. They have all addressed the same topic. This problem has been going on for years and is still happening here in the United States of America. They point out people who are very intelligent—people who have a college degree and who are very smart in that field but are just alone illiterate when it comes to being deprived of learning and mastering this information, understanding the difference between emotion and logic, following logical common sense, and thinking way out of the scale of the <u>BOX</u>.

This shows how our education system has been affected. This has had devastating effects on our country due to the deterioration of our infrastructure.

You are a very smart and intelligent person. You need to add this knowledge to your life and family. You will be amazed at the happy, humorous, and prospering rewards that this will bring into you and your family's life.

Do your Home Work: Get a second opinion: Do your research: Compare your options: Do you have a plan?

.

Prayer

People say their prayers every day asking their God for something—guidance, protection, material things, and forgiveness. Because no one is perfect, we make mistakes.

There is a movie out on DVD. In the movie, the main character can see a short amount of time into his path of life's future.

For example, he is driving a car, and his car is hit by a train. He is shown this ahead of time, which means this will happen, but it just hasn't happened yet. He has the opportunity to change the outcome. He increases the speed of the car he is driving. The train barely misses from hitting his car while driving across the railroad tracks.

He explains to you while you are watching the movie that since you have seen this event before it happens, then the event starts to change the outcome because you have seen it before it actually happens.

Starting at a young age, while he is asleep, he sees himself leaving home while riding his bicycle to school on the same path he always takes from home to school. He wants to get to school early, so he can spend time with his girlfriend before class starts. There is one intersection with a stop sign where he has to cross the street. The road has a slight curve to it. This is a problem to see cars coming from a distance. The cars have to slow down and stop for or at the stop sign.

As usual, riding his bike to school being a daily routine, he is in a hurry. He comes to the intersection and proceeds to pedal his bike through because he does not see any oncoming cars or trucks. All of a sudden, there is a car out of nowhere. He finds himself only seeing the front grill of the car. Then he feels the car thrust against his waist. Now he realizes the car is running over him as he feels his body rolling over and over under the car. All of a sudden, he wakes up. His heart is pounding out of his chest as sweat rolls down his face with his mouth wide open and with his eyes as big as they can be. He is checking to see if he is still alive. He pats himself down very quickly to see if he still has his arms, hands, legs, fingers, and toes. He jumps out of bed, runs to the bathroom, and flips on the light to see if there is any blood on him.

The shock and fear starts to fade. There is no blood and no broken bones. It is nighttime, and he is in his house still in awe as to what just happened. This happened on a Saturday night.

On Sunday morning, he is getting ready to go to church with his family. While at church, a stranger walks up to him and says, "Young man, you look as though you are scared or confused about something. Would you like to tell me about it?" The boy is not sure what to say.

The stranger says, "That's okay. You see, sometimes things happen we least expect. Also, we may see things that are way out from ordinary. So we try to figure out what to do. Pay attention to these things, and try to figure them out. Or simply ignore it."

The boy bursts out "I do not want to ignore it!" with an emotional, loud, and scared tone of voice as his eyes are filled with tears.

The stranger asks, "Why not?"

The boy takes a big swallow as tears roll down his face. "Because I am going to die!" he says as he wipes the tears from his face.

The stranger says, "Well, let's talk about it. Do you want to die?"

The boy says "Oh, no, sir" as he continues to wipe the rolling tears from his face.

"Tell me. I will keep this just between you and me, okay?"

With a glow on his face, a huge smile, and shining eyes, he raises his eyebrows and replies, "Yes, sir. Last night, while I was asleep, I was pedaling my bike to school. I came to this intersection. I looked both ways. There were no cars coming my way. So I proceeded to go through the intersection when all of a sudden, there is this car that came out of nowhere. It hits me and drives over my body as I felt myself rolling underneath the car. This is a nightmare. I do not understand. I don't want to die."

"Well, young man, you are here at church. Did you stop to think that God has heard your prayers? He is trying to protect and keep you safe."

With a concerned look on his face, he pulls down his eyebrows. "No, sir, I did not look at this that way."

"Well, son"—with a slight grin and raised eyebrow—"God may be trying to tell you that you are going to be at a certain place in a range of time. Do you know of a better way that he can answer your prayers?" he says with raised eyebrows and a slight tilt of the head.

With a surprised look on his face, eyes wide open, and a delighted smile, he says, "No, sir."

"So when these things happen, pay very close attention. Replay the event in your mind and see what you can do to change the outcome. In the long run, everything will be just fine. God helps us, but we need to help ourselves." As his eyes sparkle, he smiles. He reaches his hand over to shake his hand. The young man shakes hands with the stranger.

"Thank you, sir, for your time and help. And now I have a better understanding." The facial glow intensifies. His eyes start to twinkle as his smile grows larger on his face.

"Thank you. The second most important thing: you need to get home. I need to be on my way to help someone else."

His parents call his name. He turns to see his parents wave their arms to go. He nods his head to his parents to tell them okay. Then he turns back around to say thank you one more time and say goodbye to the very nice man. To his surprise, he is no longer there. It's as if he just disappeared.

For the rest of the day, he is replaying in his mind what he first calls a nightmare because he is viewing it emotionally. With what the stranger explained to him, he chose to view the scary event while he was asleep as an advanced notice. Here he is thinking logically.

The next day, he wakes and gets dressed. He eats breakfast, grabs his lunch, gets on his bike, and pedals toward school with concern and caution. As he approaches the intersection, he stops. He hears a low roaring sound and turns his head toward the car in the road. In a flash, he sees the car that hit him and ran over him in his sleep and run to the stop sign at a high rate of speed. *Whoosh.* The car was gone. He just sits there on his bike looking up to the sky saying "Thank you, Lord" as his face glows with a huge smile while shaking his head yes.

"God heard my prayers. Thank you."

He thinks only a few minutes had gone by. Actually, many minutes have gone by. Then he proceeds to school. He is late. His teacher is scolding him, letting him know he is in big trouble because today is a major test day. Emotionally, he could get upset by the teacher's reprimand. Logically, he takes the reprimand with ease because the main reward outweighed the reprimand. The teacher displays bold authority and loudly asks him why he was late. "Sir, I would be happy to tell you. But there is a strong possibility you will not believe me, sir."

Do your Home Work: Get a second opinion: Do your research: Compare your options: Do you have a plan?

How Would You Like to Learn a Surefire Way to Accomplish Your Goals?

I learned the Serenity of Prayer and "ask and you shall receive" as a child during a vacation Bible school. I listened while the pastor was discussing it, and he gave his interpretation. What I found confusing was listening to the people of the congregation after church. As everyone gathered for social visiting after church services were over, they were scoffing at the services. Because as they discussed among the surrounding people, they made the same comment many times that they have prayed and asked God for many things, but little to nothing showed up. To my amazement, many people all said the same thing.

My first thought to me, myself, and I: there has to be something missing. Or there must be a combination like a combination lock. You have to do something in an order. But what is the combination to open this lock? As per my grandfather's words: the answer is right in front of you!

I remember when I said my prayer and asked God, "I know you're busy helping other prayers. Is it possible you can send someone to me? That can explain 'ask and you will receive' Serenity of Prayer." It was in a form of language that an eight-year-old boy can easily understand. "Thank you, sir, for your time."

The following Sunday, after service, a woman walked up and asked if I wanted to learn a secret. "Yes, ma'am. Of course I would!"

"Well, young man, it is very important to understand. All you have to do is…"

My eyebrows were up and my eyes wide open with excitement. Was this an answer to my prayer?

"Yes, ma'am. Yes, ma'am. I am listening." All of a sudden, my parents were calling me by name to leave and go home. I was in great suspense. I tried to stall for time. I was close. The woman tilted her head, raised her shoulders, and smiled.

"I guess you will have to wait until the following Sunday to learn the rest."

I stood there in such high suspense, gritted my teeth, shook my head back and forth, and stomped my feet on the ground.

"Yes, ma'am. Thank you, ma'am, with a long next Sunday! Bye, ma'am."

During the week, the suspense was really taking a toll on me. I was becoming crabby and forgetting my manners. My grandmother noticed this in my actions. She confronted me of this unusual behavior. "Grandson, why are you acting the way you are? Constantly asking what day it is."

"Grandmother, I said a prayer. I think the prayer was answered. But I am in great suspense because of the interruption that took place. Now I have to wait until this coming Sunday to find out the rest of the secret. Plus wondering if that same woman is going to be there."

"What woman, son?"

"I don't know her name."

"What does she look like?"

So I described her. I watched my grandmother's eyebrows come down. Her eyes shifted from side to side, and she had a straight facial expression. All of a sudden, her eyebrows shot up. Her eyes widened, then she smiled. "Tell your grandfather I will be right back."

"Yes, ma'am. There he is right over there." We both watched her run into the house and come out with her purse and jumped into her car and created a lot of dust from her tires as she sped away. My grandfather hurried over to me.

"What is going on with great concern?"

"Sir, she told me to tell you she will be right back, sir."

"As fast as she was moving, you would think the house is on fire."

"Yes, sir. I agree I have never seen her move that fast in a hurry."

"I'll have a talk with that woman when she gets back. You can be sure of that!"

"Yes, sure," I replied as I looked to see his neck and face turn red while trying to roll a cigarette with his hands shanking.

*****

Few hours passed. My grandfather and I were sitting on an overturned aluminum boat. I was listening to him tell me about events of his early days. From there, we watched my grandmother pull up to the house in a hurry.

"Son, stay put. I got some words to say to your grandmother," he said as he got up and started walking toward her. She got out of the car and started walking toward us.

"Old man, I need to talk to you right now!"

"Woman, are you trying to scare the dickens out of me? And years cannot spare? What's going on? Why did you leave in on all fired up hurry?"

My grandparents walked toward each other until they met halfway. My grandfather, in great concern and suspense wearing his big black cowboy hat, raised both arms with hands wide open.

"What is going on here?" My grandmother's hands were on each hip.

"Shut up and listen!"

All of a sudden, it was like they were whispering because I can no longer hear them talking. I did notice my grandmother poking my grandfather in the chest as she shook her head from side to side. Then slowly, I watched both of them turned and looked directly at me. I didn't know what to think. It looked like I was in some kind of trouble. But I didn't do anything to be in trouble, for that I know of.

All of a sudden, my grandparents embraced in a loving, caring hug. This lasted for more than just several seconds. When they parted, you could see my grandmother dried the tears from her eyes. I watched as my grandfather brought his hand up to his face.

My grandmother walked to the house. My grandfather walked back to sit down and didn't say a word. I looked at him only to see his neck and face were still red, and why were his eyes full of tears? I was getting upset. My eyes were filling full of tears because I did not understand why my grandfather was so upset! We sat there for a few more minutes not saying a word and were just wiping tears from our eyes. He turned and looked at me as he was wiping his tears from his eyes. "Son, there is something I have to do. So let's just go in the house. We will finish this at a later time."

"Yes, sir, let's go." As he put his arm around my shoulder, we walked to the house. I still didn't know the secret, or I will get to learn it and get prepared for what tomorrow will bring.

Several days went by. Each day, I was expecting to listen to my grandfather tell me of his adventures only to find him quiet in the house reading his Bible with a very little to say to me.

Then came Saturday. He taught me a life lesson that day. While we were sitting down for breakfast, I noticed my grandfather reached into the cabinet and pulled out a handful of cinnamon suckers. Then he put them into his shirt pocket. Naturally, I knew that he would share and give me one. "You need to stay with me all day long."

"Yes, sir."

"First we will ride out to the thirty acres field to see if the water is in the irrigation ditch for watering."

"Yes, sir." Now I couldn't help but notice my grandfather slowly pulled out one of the cinnamon suckers from his shirt pocket. He just held it in front of himself looking at it very carefully. He took the wrapper off it then put into his mouth and showed emotion and sounds with facial expressions on how good it tasted.

I was expecting him to offer me one.

But to my surprise, he did not. I asked him if I could have one. He just ignored me. I knew he had a hard time hearing, but I did not whisper when I asked for one. I just sat there very disappointed. Now I know that my grandfather played mind games. He had been doing this to make you think outside the box. If I did not know better, I would think he was taunting me. So I figured I will just play along to see if I can figure out what he was up to.

As the days went by, he continued to eat sucker after sucker right in front of me. Not once did he offer me one even though I have asked him for one more than once. I was almost at the point I did not want one, maybe.

Most of the day had gone by. My grandfather told me he needed to talk to me when we got back to the farm.

My grandfather and I were sitting in front of the barn on the overturned flat bottom boat. "Son, I need to tell you about people. People will want all kind of things throughout their lives. But when it comes to prayers, asking God, they forget that he answers their prayers. One thing that they ask for do not always show up overnight. Plus the things they ask for do not always show up in the manner in which they can relate to.

"For example, there is a major hurricane that hits a city. There are high winds and massive flooding. This individual, man or woman, is trapped in their home due to the rising floodwaters. They managed to get out of the house and up on the rooftop of their house to escape the rising water. Here this is the highest place they can get. Plus they know someone can see them and help them to safety. Now this individual says their prayers to their God asking, 'Please, God, rescue me and take me to safety. There is only a few hours of daylight left.' To their amazement, they see a man in a canoe paddling toward their house. The man in the canoe lands his canoe on the rooftop of the house. 'Get in. I am here to rescue you and take you to safety.' The individual says, 'No, thank you. I am waiting for my God to rescue me.' The man in the canoe leaves away. Soon after, a man in a flat bottom boat with a motor and other people he has rescued pulls up to the same rooftop of the individual. 'We are here to rescue you and take you to safety. Get in the boat.' The individual says, 'No. My God will rescue me and take me to safety.' The captain of the motorboat leaves.

"It is dark now. A helicopter is flying above, patrolling, looking for survivors. With the spotlight, they see the individual on the rooftop of their house, just waving their arms. Now the floodwaters are still rising rapidly. The helicopter hovers directly overhead of the individual and lowers the ladder down to them and tells the individual by using a speakerphone to grab the ladder and climb up. 'We are here to rescue you and take you to safety.' The individual says, 'No, thanks. My God will rescue me and take me to safety.' The helicopter flies away. The floodwaters keep rising. The individual perished in the rising floodwater.

"When a gift is given to them by means of their prayers, they don't even say thank you because it does not fit the picture in their mind. They turn it down! They ask for a gift. It shows up, and they ignore it and walk away! They turn it down!

"The gift can show up right in front of them, and they don't even realize it because they were not looking for what they had asked for. They were not looking for what they had asked for. They turned it down. Think about a parent when their child asked to get them a gift. They get it. Don't say thank you. Complain, show no appreciation, and turn it down. How many times are the parents going to put up with that? They ask for another gift?

"How long should a parent keep doing that? Now who will get it for them?"

During the time he was lecturing, I watched him enjoying the sweet flavor of the cinnamon sucker. I noticed that he had four more suckers in his shirt pocket. I figured he would offer me one to enjoy during his lecture. But to my surprise, he did not.

I watched him eat one sucker, pulled out another, and began to eat as well. Still, he didn't offer me one. Later in the lecture, my grandfather, with the heel of his boot, started to stomp or dig in a small hole in the ground where we were sitting. This small hole in the ground was right between his left and right boots. After eating the suckers, my grandfather started to enjoy his chewing tobacco. Each time he had a mouth full of tobacco spit, he would spit in the small hole in the ground between his boots. Now it did not take long for this hole to be filled up with tobacco spit.

I finally asked him if he was going to give me a cinnamon sucker or share since he still had some in his shirt pocket. He just looked at me. "Now if you were saying a prayer asking for a cinnamon sucker, what would you say?"

Now I knew my grandfather was testing me. So I proceeded to ask in prayer aloud, "Lord, is it possible for someone sitting close to me to share and offer me a cinnamon sucker that is in his shirt pocket? AMEN."

My grandfather pulled a cinnamon sucker out of his pocket. The sucker had a dirty bent stick, and this was normally a clean straight white stick. It is wrapped in newspaper. Normally, it was wrapped in clean plastic.

Then he dropped the sucker right into the puddle of tobacco spit. I was very surprised, let down, and felt hurt. There, for a few seconds, I was thinking, *am I going to reject this sucker submerged in tobacco spit?* I looked at my grandfather with a hasty facial expression on my face.

I saw him trying very hard not to laugh. His eyes sparkled. His eyebrows were up with this funny smile. Well? Then I recalled that this was a test to see if I was paying attention to his lecture. I tried to keep from smiling, but that did not work. I just smiled as I watched him smile. Thank you.

"Thank you, Lord, for answering my prayers of asking for someone close to me to share his cinnamon suckers with me."

In reality, what did I ask for?

I leaned down, picked up the sucker, the one with the dirty bent stick which was wrapped in newspaper, lying submerged in tobacco spit. I took it into the barn, washed off the tobacco spit, took off the newspaper wrapping, washed off the dirty bent stick, and proceeded to enjoy eating the sweet cinnamon sucker. The one I had asked for in prayer was given.

My grandfather taught psychology and philosophy though he didn't have a diploma. I have compiled this booklet in order to guide everyone toward their goals in life—even those which may seem impossible.

I have used these same principles and compiled them so that you can be a success. They work! You were the only one who stopped you from success in whatever you set for goals in your personal and professional life.

After you have completed reading *The Big Secret: A Parent's Treasure,* sure go back and read again. Use it as you set your goal and work toward it.

You don't need luck. You need to be dedicated to what you want to accomplish!

Do your Home Work: Get a second opinion: Do your research: Compare your options: Do you have a plan?

What Exactly is This All About?

What EXACTLY are the BASIC PRINCIPLE RULES OF LIFE?

This book is a simple tool to help you along your journey. It is a self-guided thinking tool. This is good for leadership, for testing yourself, and for helping guide you in constructing a plan—often a proposal or intended course of action. This guide challenges your self-esteem and improves your courage. This guided tool, when used properly, will automatically orchestrate PLAN *A* and PLAN *B*.

The men raising the flag on the cover tell you everything you need to know. You just don't know it yet! They can be positive, can be encouraging, and can motivate you to success. These strong, brave men and this book, if used properly, can help you achieve outstanding results and aid you in accomplishing your goals. I live in this success story. I know it works, and I know it changes life—it did change mine!

Let me begin with a story that will show you how my Basic Principle Rules of Life came to fruition. These "basic principles" made it possible for me to accomplish goal after goal, and they continue to do so!

All through my school years, I was just an average student making average grades and sustaining an average grade point average (GPA). During my senior year in high school, there was an announcement that all graduating seniors were to sit according to their GPA rather than alphabetically at graduation.

Therefore, if you carried a high GPA, then your name would be among the first ones to be announced. If you carried an average

GPA, then you would be announced somewhere in the middle. And if you carried a low GPA, your name would be announced at the end.

There were 327 graduating seniors in my class. After the first nine weeks of school, the office staff posted a seating arrangement according to each student's GPA. I believed my name would be found somewhere in the middle to upper half of this arrangement.

WOW. Was I ever shocked, embarrassed, and humiliated to see my name at the 320 spot, which was seventh from the bottom!

At this point, it was evident that my slacking off at school with a "just-get-by" attitude making grades that were just above passing had come back to seriously bit me in the rear.

I decided to give myself a challenge. During the remaining twenty-seven weeks of school, I wanted to see just how far I could move up the seating arrangement. I set this goal for myself because I knew no one else would do it for me.

Do your Home Work: Get a second opinion: Do your research: Compare your options: Do you have a plan?

Quotes to Read Before Completing Simple Step-by-Step Instructions for Using and Applying the Basic Principle Rules of Life

- Have faith in who you are, where you are going, where you came from, and who you represent. The rewards can be astronomical.
- Simply show your appreciation, and always say "Thank you."
- Don't think you are not good enough to receive a gift or award. You are good enough, and you do deserve it.
- Be positive, be supportive, and be encouraging. Help the other person enhance his/her outlook.
- You are free to like yourself, be happy with yourself, and be proud of yourself. You are free to think and act positively and discharge the negative.
- If it is worth doing, then do it right now.
- Ask for feedback, and then refine yourself.
- Be the best you can be. You have to live with yourself.
- Choose your own destiny. Don't rely on someone else.
- Compete against yourself to achieve more than you can imagine.
- Patience is a virtue, but persistence to the point of success is a blessing.

- Be proud of the degree you earned from the University of Hard Knocks. Sometimes, that degree will override a college degree.
- Using great manners with great respect will earn you a tremendous hand of help.
- Come up with a plan to accomplish success. A Dream! An idea! Set a goal!
- Accomplish a goal by observing each step because there is a science. You have succeeded in your plan this far. Now you need to finish the goal.
- To accomplish success, put one foot in front of the other.
- It is not what is on the platter. It is how you present it.
- When given a choice, take both.
- If anything goes wrong, fix it.
- Start at the top, and then work your way up.
- It is best to talk to people who know what they are talking about when doing research because they have credibility.
- Keep a positive attitude when you are criticized or put down, and ask that person to teach you a better way.
- Don't believe in a stranger before believing in someone you know.
- Things work out when you least expect it.
- Facing and confronting the unknown will allow you to acquire knowledge and rewards.
- There is honor in victory, but putting forth the effort is also victory.
- "No" simply means not right now.
- Begin a level higher.
- When asked an open question, ask for a specific, so you can answer a closed question.
- Do not answer a question if you do not know what the question is asking.
- When scared or confused, shut your mouth.
- Think about the question before you answer it.
- Knowledge is power—only if you need it and use it.

- Learn the system, and more doors will open than you can imagine.
- Learn common sense, then master it, then rejoice in it.
- Learn when it is the best time to be a good listener.
- To accomplish success, you have to put it in motion.
- Don't walk when you can run.
- Face your fears with fear to succeed.
- Learn to speak and think on multiple levels.
- You need to know when to hold.
- You need to know when to buy.
- You need to know when to sell.
- You need to know when to fold.
- You need to be able to sense when it is time to leave.
- Don't think or act like Chicken Little.
- Stop, think, take the time to investigate, and go to all the main sources to find out and learn the facts.
- Hearsay and assumptions will cost you dearly.
- Don't miss out on rewards of life by trying to make everything perfect.
- Do not underestimate your capabilities toward success.
- It is who you know with what you know.
- Take one step at a time.
- Keep it simple.
- To think outside your box, you must dismantle your box for eternity.
- The more you open yourself, the more you will find.
- Don't be afraid to address someone who has a higher working status.
- You are free to choose when you are the boss and at what time who rules.
- You are free to learn all you want.
- You are the main one stopping yourself.
- When in doubt, think creatively, and use imagination with logic.
- Multiple projects lead to multiple success.

- Do not give up your goal because someone is more successful than you.
- Perfection is not an option.
- Keep a good attitude of optimism.
- Do not view things through a tunnel.
- Do not become a procrastinator.
- Do not become a pessimist.
- Do not become a dreamer or a want-to-be.
- Do not underestimate your completion.
- The ones you admire the most will aid you toward your success.
- Do not be afraid of rejection.
- The ones you fear the least can be the ones to destroy you.
- Hard knocks—best teacher.
- Be prepared for someone to throw a wrench in your gears of motion.
- Don't just listen. Pay very close attention!
- Don't just look. Observe.
- Facing and confronting something you fear could turn out to be your best friends.
- When confronting an issue, do your homework and research.
- Learn as soon as you can that logical decisions override emotional decisions.
- When forced to compromise, think with pure logic.
- Master the art of convincing others that what they believe may not be true.
- When you run into an obstacle, stop and rethink your plan. There is another way.
- People make the same mistakes many times. Decide not to be one of them.
- On the road of a life of success, if you get knocked down, get up and try again.
- Don't be afraid to learn something new.
- Do not be offended by constructive criticism.
- Be prepared of jealousy from others because of your success.

- If you are in the wrong, acknowledge it, and face up to the issue with dignity.
- Learn something new. Change can be good.
- Do not spread yourself too thin.
- Don't be afraid to ask questions.
- If you can't beat them, join them, and then beat them.
- Bureaucracy is a challenge to be conquered with a righteous attitude and tolerance.
- Remember your legal rights.
- Do not talk over someone because the person may know more than you.
- You can be "scared straight."
- Consider the realistic consequences of your behavior before you act.
- Don't live in denial that bad things won't happen to you.
- The more you worry about other people's problems, the more problems you have to worry about.
- Do not frown on ignorance.
- Knowledge is power—only if you need it and know how to use it.
- Decide that you will succeed in everything you do.

Simple Step-by-Step Instructions for Using and Applying the Basic Principle Rules of Life

Think with an open mind and not with a foolish one.

Ask three people to give you an opinion to the same question or quote.

My question is this: would all three people give the same answers? The answer is NO! Those people are raised differently, are influenced by different people, and have different events happen during their lifetimes!

When you use your computer and you want to have your computer capability to increase its memory, then you add more memory, right?

Your BRAIN is just like a computer. So if you want to be capable of thinking SMARTER than working HARDER, you need to do this exercise to add this to your brain's "program."

The GREAT thing about this is that you achieve prosperity, your courage becomes stronger, and you find your self-esteem much higher than it ever was!

Do you understand the outcome? Take these steps and you will.

There are many people who are very successful, and you want to be just as successful or even more than those you admire. It has been proven in statistics!

The people who become very successful have done this REPETITION—"repeating or being repetitive" or "something done or said again," which means you "repeat." Follow the same steps as the person you want to be like or in the same field you want to be successful in.

All of the people in the success stories in this book worked at jobs, probably like the one you are doing now, and likely made the same amount of money you make. In fact, they may have been working right next to you!

Maybe their vehicle was nearly worn out like yours might be. But these people now have success stories because they did something you have not done yet. They made a conscious effort to improve their lives.

They took this first step. They sat down, focused, and wrote down the first of these quotes which were listed on pages <<Note to layout: insert page number here>>. Then they added not one, not two, but three of their own definitions explaining what they feel that quote meant to them. They were also able to use the quote in different ways.

Then they did the same thing with the second quote, the third, and then on the more than one hundred of them making it now three hundred!

Why did the successful people that I talked about in this book accomplish their goals? Because they followed this plan of success! They read, learned, and followed the "Big Secret!"

You will accomplish the same successes and can achieve even more than they did if you follow these steps and believe you can make more of yourself!

So let's get started. Prepare to challenge yourself, and prove to yourself that you can do it!

I Did It! Let Me Show You How!

But I needed an executable plan. I began making a list of "Basic Principle Rules of Life" that would be easy to follow and that could easily serve as a guide. I sat down one afternoon and began to brainstorm on what I could do to accomplish this goal.

The following list was the result of that brainstorming session that applied to my goal in my senior year in high school:

- Do your homework.
- Do more than what you are required to do—read ahead a few chapters.
- Ask for extra credit work.
- Do not be afraid to ask for help.
- Show appreciation by saying "Thank you."
- Learn how the teachers are teaching their classes and grading the assignments or tests.
- Learn to use common sense.
- Learn how to face and confront the unknown.
- Face the fears of success.
- Take everything one step at a time.
- Keep it simple.
- Do not underestimate your own capabilities.
- Do not think you are not good enough to receive recognition, a gift, or a reward.
- Realize that you are free to think positive, and disregard all negative.
- You are free to like yourself, be happy with yourself, and be proud of yourself.
- Believe knowledge is power, and use it when you need to.
- Put the plan into action—you can do it!

Yes, sure. This is a lot of work! But imagine at the age of sixteen, seventeen, or eighteen practicing for your future and using these principles throughout your life! You will discover that it will be something you use all the time in everything you do!

Once I finished the list, I put it in order of importance, and at this point, a plan was established. I began executing the plan and began using it as my "Basic Principle Rules of Life." As I applied these basic principles, my GPA began to increase.

In fact, I had no idea just how quickly my grades were improving. I became a member of the National Honor Society, and my name moved to number six on the seating arrangement for the graduation! This increase was a 321-point jump!

At the last minute, just before the students with the highest GPAs signed the senior board, I learned I would be signing the board in the number one spot! I had moved up another five spots from number six to number one.

I had set a goal for myself, constructed a plan, and put that plan into action by applying the "Basic Principle Rules of Life."

The moral to this short story is that out of 327 graduating seniors, I started at number 320, climbed my way up to number six then to number one by following those principles in my senior year. Therefore, I graduated at the top of my class as cum laude in 1976.

Do your Home Work: Get a second opinion: Do your research: Compare your options: Do you have a plan?

A Tidbit of Trivia

Back in 1976, when a student graduated from high school, his or her grade point average was very close to that of a college sophomore.

In 1977, the government lowered the grade point average for a student to graduate. The results of this decision were devastating. Graduating seniors who took the SATs and ACTs were not scoring high enough for college acceptance.

Therefore, colleges had to lower the test scores, so students were able to pass and gain college acceptance!

Think about it. Do public schools teach their students common sense or how to use it? Do they teach their students to think outside of the box or how to think outside of the box? If you wish to regain what schools used to teach, then this guide on the "Basic Principle Rules of Life" will definitely be the tool to accomplish this goal.

Teaching Others How to Apply the "Basic Principle Rules of Life"

As a den leader for my son's Cub Scouts troop, I taught the boys the "Basic Principle Rules of Life" by helping them learn and showing them the following:

o   How to use common sense.
o   How to be aware of their surroundings.
o   How to use their imagination.
o   How to think creatively.
o   How to set goals.
o   How to come up with a plan to accomplish their goals.
o   How to find answer to their own questions by asking them what they felt they wanted to know.
o   Giving them a positive environment.
o   Giving them encouragement.
o   Showing them motivation.
o   And telling them "Yes, you can" and letting them know that "cannot" is not an option!

The boys loved this and did very well learning it. Their parents were a whole other story.

They got together to discuss the way I led the troop, and they asked me to step down from being a leader to an assistant.

The parents appointed another den leader, and all the boys threw a fight, which made me feel proud. The boys told the new den leader how much they missed me and how they wished I were still the leader. The parents came to regret their decision and came to me to apologize for their decision. Each of them admitted they were jealous and intimidated and felt like failures as parents because they should have been the ones teaching their own kids about the "Basic Principle Rules of Life."

All of the boys' parents apologized profusely and asked me to take back over as den leader, so I could continue teaching their boys. They said they were sorry for acting so abruptly without giving any thought to how their actions would affect their boys. I accepted their apologies and told them not to worry because they could not teach their boys what they themselves did not know.

It is sad because this shows, years later, what was taken out of schools and how it affects the American people even today.

Do your Home Work: Get a second opinion: Do your research: Compare your options: Do you have a plan?

What's the Big Secret?

I am sure you were asking, "What is the big secret?" Two adults and eight kids kept this secret silent for more than thirty years. Let me tell you how I came to learn this important information.

My grandparents had their own business. They ran and operated a self-sufficient dairy farm. Mom and Dad worked outside their home, so when I came into this world, my parents would take me to the dairy farm and leave me with Aunt Sue.

She was my main caregiver fulfilling the role of "Mom." The Christmas when I was four, Aunt Sue and her husband, Uncle Pete, adopted a three-year-old girl.

This was confusing to me because all of a sudden, there was another child in the picture, and this child was not a baby but a kid like me. I asked Aunt Sue how this girl could be her daughter since she did not have her as a baby. She sat me down and explained in a way a four-year-old would comprehend as to what an adoption was and how it worked. She explained that she and Uncle Pete had a lot of love to give not only to each other but to a little child as well.

I spent most of my time helping Aunt Sue with her daily tasks around the farm. I helped her wash clothes in an outdated washing machine which had hand crank rollers to wring water out of the clothes. Once the water was out of the clothes, I helped her put the clean wet clothes into a laundry basket, and she carried the basket outside to the clothesline.

One day, I noticed her straining in pain as she lifted the heavy laundry basket full of wet clothes. Even though I was only a child, I knew this was a painful way for her to handle her job. Thanks to the way I had been raised, I used my reasoning and knew there had to be a better way.

I must have startled her when I yelled at her to stop. She looked at me with a surprised look on her face and asked why. I ran out of the laundry room proud of myself for using things that I had been taught even at that young age.

I pulled in my brand-new wagon, my Christmas present that year, and announced that she would no longer have to carry the heavy laundry basket full of wet clothes from the house to the clothesline. She looked at me with a sparkle in her eye and a half smile on her face and said, "So you think if we put this heavy laundry basket in your red wagon then pull the wagon out to the clothesline, I won't hurt my back?"

I nodded and said, "Yes, ma'am."

She replied, "Sounds like you got a plan, so let's do it!"

Later on that day, I tripped and fell, tearing my pants and cutting my knee. I was wailing because it hurt and because I was afraid I might get into trouble for tearing my pants. Aunt Sue picked me up, dusted off my pants, and carried me inside. The entire time she cleaned and doctored my knee, she was trying to calm me down by talking softly telling me not to worry about my pants because they could be fixed as good as new. As she dried my eyes, she said, "You are big boy, and you need to take on the responsibility of being a bit more careful."

Later that day, lo and behold, my aunt Sue took a tumble in front of the house while she was carrying a box. She banged and scraped her knee just as I had, and she was in tremendous pain.

I told her, "Now you just sit still, and I will be right back."

She protested saying that she needed to go take care of her knee.

I replied, "No, Aunt Sue. I am a big boy now. You just sit right there, and I will tend to your wound." I ran inside to get a wet rag, antibiotic ointment, and bandages. I ran back outside and reassured her that sometimes accidents just can't be helped.

I told her that crying does not make the pain go away or make the wound feel better. (Ah, the wisdom of a child but a child who had been taught how to think!) Tears ran down her face, and I felt sad that she was in such pain. Because I was only four years old, I had no idea she was really crying not because her knee was hurting but because of the pride and elation my actions of humility and responsibility caused.

She could not believe that I turned around and took care of her as she had taken care of me when I fell earlier that day. She gave me a big bear hug, and I asked her if she would be my mom. That made her hug me even tighter and caused her to cry even more.

Well, now I started crying because I could not figure out why she was so upset. She wiped away my tears and then her own and said, "I would like very much to be your mom, but you know, you already have one."

I replied, "What difference does that make? I have two grandmothers and two grandfathers. They both do the same thing, so why can't I have two moms? Besides, you explained adoption to me at Christmas. So if I adopt you as my mom, will you adopt me as your son? If you do this, then you will have a son and a daughter to look after, and you are doing that anyway!"

Aunt Sue looked at me in an odd, peculiar, and, I am sure, very surprised way. She knew I had made a great point and was correct. But she tried to explain that if she were to allow me to call her mom, it would cause a lot of trouble, especially with my mom and dad. My other relatives would be upset as well, she tried to explain to me.

I thought about what she had said and then asked if we could keep it "our little secret." She finally agreed but only if I didn't tell anyone else. In my best serious little boy voice, I promised. But I wanted her to understand that I was serious, and our secret meant something special to me—something "official." She asked how we could do that, and I got down on one knee. Even today, I can still recall the words I used. I said, "Aunt Sue, I want to adopt you as my mom."

She smiled and replied, "I accept!" In turn, she got down on her good knee and said, "I want to adopt you, James, as my son."

I answered, "Yes, ma'am. I accept." Lo and behold, this is how the "secret" started!

As time passed by, "Mom" as Aunt Sue went from raising one child all the way to raising eight. She had four girls of her own plus two nephews and two nieces whom she also raised as her own.

And my mom had four kids: two boys and two girls. Over the years, we eight kids dealt with all the usual issues kids get along with and squabble about. One biggie decided who the "boss" was.

Initially, since I was the oldest, I agreed to be the boss. But over time, we decided it would be best to take turns. Each day, we would rotate, so everyone got a chance to be the boss of our group. We even decided to take it a step further and arrange it, so our group did things using parliamentary procedures. We elected president, vice president, secretary, and sergeant at arms.

But we soon found out it was not going to work out very well since there were four titles and there were eight of us. We decided to do away with the parliamentary procedures and become a "council." One day, we were all together getting ready to eat lunch when Aunt Sue (now my second mom) announced, "We will be going into town after lunch."

I slipped and addressed her as "Mom" in front of my brother and cousins. There was a shocking huge response from the other kids. To hear me call Aunt Sue "Mom" was totally unacceptable. There was no end to the grief I received after that mishap. Trust me, I got an earful! The six girls were very upset, so I told them that we would hold a special council meeting before we went into town.

During the council meeting, each of Aunt Sue's four girls pro-ceeded to voice their opinion one at a time saying, "James, she is our mom. You already have a mom." My two cousins spoke up agreeing with the girls. My brother was the voice of reason.

He said, "Hang on. Let James explain why he called Aunt Sue 'Mom.'"

Imagine this little boy standing up and telling the others why it all made sense to me. I explained that we all had two grandmothers and two grandfathers. I told them that both sets of grandparents had the same role: they taught us, guided us, cared for us, and cuddled with us. Because they took on the roles in our lives—both sets—in a way, they fulfilled the role of parents. Since that made sense, why was it that we couldn't have two moms?

I explained that the way I saw it. Our mom had to work, so Aunt Sue, as our caregiver, had assumed the role of our mother. The only time we saw our mother and spent time with her was in the evenings when she came to pick us up and take us home. Even then, all we had time for was getting our baths, putting our pajamas on, and climbing into bed.

The next day, we would get up and do it all over again. We spent most of our days at the farm with Aunt Sue as she fulfilled the role of "Mom" to each one of us who watched over us, so we do not get hurt. She taught us all we have learned. Aunt Sue had cuddled us, comforted us when we got hurt, helped us learn to use common sense, be aware of our surroundings, think outside of the box, responsibility, creative thinking, and more! Aunt Sue had been the one to do all these things.

Years later, we will each look back on this and see that because of Aunt Sue, we had a maturity level older than our younger years. She deserved all the credit for who we became and will continue to become. I told them I was proud and honored to adopt her as a mother.

In our closing discussion, my brother and two girl cousins agreed with all I had said, and they decided that they wanted to adopt her as their "mother" as well. The issue went up for a vote from the council, and all eight agreed unanimously that it would be great if my sisters, my brother, and I adopted Aunt Sue as our "mother." We agreed this decision would stay within the group of kids and should not be shared with other relatives. After a night of everyone thinking it over, the council reconvened to discuss this further and make a final decision.

The next day, we held our council meeting while Mom (Aunt Sue) waited in suspense for the outcome. Everyone had thought it over and decided that it made sense, and it was easy to come to a logical decision. We were all in agreement. Yes, there was definitely nothing wrong with us having two "moms," and it would be best if each of us kept this quiet and not reveal it to the other relatives. Therefore, we put it to a vote and agreed unanimously that this "adoption" of Aunt Sue would be our secret. We shared our decision with her, and with tears in our eyes, we all came together with open arms into one huge, united group hug, which made it all official.

As the years passed, some things happened which can be described as sad yet a blessing in disguise. "Mom" (Aunt Sue) went through a divorce and later met a man named Mike. He was a happy-go-lucky kind of guy, and because he loved her so much, he was willing to take on the responsibility of helping her raise her four daughters as his own. While they were dating and getting to know each other, Mike showed up at the farm one morning offering to help his future wife and in-laws with chores. He was startled to see not four girls but six and two boys. He pulled her aside and asked if there was something she forgot to mention or if she was going to wait until after they were married to spring it on him that she actually had eight kids instead of four. He reminded her that she had said she had four girls, and he was fine with that, but he saw eight kids at the farm that day.

He asked how many kids she "really had." He wondered if maybe there might be more next time he came to see her.

"I mean, tomorrow, am I going to see ten kids on the farm? I would like an answer now."

Well, I stepped up and said, "Mr. Mike, sir, if you spare ten to fifteen minutes, you will get your answers."

Then I turned and hollered that there would be a council meeting in fifteen seconds. All eight of us kids, along with "Mom" (Aunt Sue), huddled up to discuss this issue. We all loved Mike. He was positive, encouraging, and just a great guy to be around with, and none of us wanted to see him walk out. We decided the only way to handle this situation was to inform him of the BIG SECRET, so we came up with a PLAN.

It was lunchtime, so we decided that each kid, one at a time, would carry an item, give it to Mike, and ask him the "question." The youngest, Bobby, went first carrying a napkin. She handed him the napkin then asked him if she could adopt him as her father and if he would adopt her as his daughter. The look on his face was priceless!

Sabra went next, carrying a paper plate. Then Edwina went carrying half a sandwich. She was followed by Sherry carrying the other half of the sandwich. Then Tracy carried in his silverware. Zane carried a glass of tea. Darrell brought him chips, and Icame in carrying a pitcher of tea. As each one handed him the part of lunch they are carrying, they asked him if they could adopt him as their father and if he would, in turn, adopt them as his son or daughter.

He sat there with this emotional, bewildered look on his face and was completely speechless. We had all agreed to walk away and give him time to think about and to consider the question we each proposed.

As we all turned, in suspense, to walk away, he hollered, "Where is everyone going? Are you going to leave me here to eat all by myself?" Each of us stopped and turned around to find him grinning from ear to ear. He looked at "Mom" (Aunt Sue) and asked her, "Now I need to know. Are all eight of these kids yours?"

She replied quite firmly, "These four girls we will be raising all the time. As for the other four, we will be raising them half of the time. Therefore, to answer your question, yes, all eight of the kids are mine. So you can either take it or leave it, buster!" This man deserves so much credit.

He responded, "I would be proud and more than honored to be adopted by all eight of you kids. And yes, I would love to adopt each of you as my sons and my daughters."

"Dad" (Uncle Mike) had a PLAN to use a piece of machinery to pull a motor and transmission out of an old truck. His father-in-law, my grandfather, told him he could not use the tractor with the front-end loader to pull the motor. As I watched this transpire, I realized the importance of having a backup PLAN.

I walked up to "Dad" (Uncle Mike) and stood quietly by his side because I could tell how mad he was, and after a moment, I asked him if he had a backup PLAN. He turned and looked at me with a proud and curious expression, and he said, "Well, I am thinking about a PLAN *B*."

I responded by telling him maybe I could help since two heads are better than one. We began reviewing the task at hand and brainstorming about an alternate PLAN. PLAN *B* was to raise the truck high enough off the ground, so we could drop the engine and transmission instead of lifting them out. Once we had them dropped, we would pull them out from underneath the body of the truck. Working together, figuring, and calculating, we were able to accomplish our goal.

In closing, many heartfelt thanks go out to my aunt Sue and uncle Mike for instilling in each of us eight kids the BASIC PRINCIPLE RULES OF LIFE. The age range for us eight was two years old to nine years old, but each of us had the mentality of teenagers because of all Aunt Sue and Uncle Mike taught us. When we were older, we gathered for another council meeting where each of us agreed on how many great and wonderful things we learned from both "Moms" and both "Dads."

Each one of them were unique and special in their own way; therefore, one was not better or more important than the other, but they were equal.

Simple Step-by-Step Instructions
to Using and Applying the
BASIC PRINCIPLE RULES OF LIFE

Step 1: For your first attempt, try to keep your goal small. By following this step, it will be easier to accomplish the next bigger goal.

Step 2: Think of a situation or an issue that you would like to improve upon, and make this your first goal. Remember to start small, and work your way to the bigger situations or issues.

Step 3: Take a piece of paper and write down your goal.

Step 4: Take a deep breath, relax, and open your mind. Read all the quotes one by one. Each time you read a quote you think may aid or solve your situation or issue, write that quote underneath where you wrote your current situation or issue and goal. By the time you have read through each quote, you may discover you have written down many of the quotes. Now worries. Do not let this send you into a panic. Just continue calmly onto the next step.

Step 5: Reread each quote you have written down, and review each one. These quotes are your constructed PLAN *A* or your rough draft, if you will.

Step 6: Study all the quotes, decide where you need the most help or assistance with, and match that with the quote that best fits what you think should be put into action first. Then continue studying the quotes deciding where you need the most help or assistance next, and match that with the quote that best fits what you think should be put into action second. Continue repeating this step.

Step 7: As you put these quotes into action, you will see you are getting closer and closer to reaching and accomplishing your first goal.

Do your Home Work: Get a second opinion: Do your research: Compare your options: Do you have a plan?

Serenity of Prayer

One day, my grandfather and I were sitting in front of the barn. He told me about how people will want all kinds of things throughout their lives. But when it comes to asking God, they forget that he answers their prayers. But the things they ask for do not always show up in the manner in which they can relate to. For example, when a gift is given to them, they don't even say thank you because it does not fit the picture in their mind. They turn it down! They ask for a gift. It shows up, and they ignore it and walk away! They turn it down!

The gift can show up right in front of them, and they don't even realize it because they are not looking for what they had asked for. They turn it down. Think about a parent when their child asks to get them a gift. They get it, don't say thank you, complain, show no appreciation, and turn it down.

How many times are they going to put up with that? Then they ask for another gift! How long should a parent keep doing that? Now who will get it for them?

Do your Home Work: Get a second opinion: Do your research: Compare your options: Do you have a plan?

Success Stories

Thomas Jefferson

The third President of the United States wrote the Declaration of Independence using words "created equal" that today are repeated over and over and which acquired the Louisiana territory. His face has been immortalized on the United States' five-cent coin. Jefferson as a boy was destined to great things after learning the importance of accomplishing your goals.

My Oldest Daughter

My oldest daughter is a young woman with an average IQ who married shortly after graduating high school. By using and applying the "BASIC PRINCIPLE RULES OF LIFE," she was able to begin her own business. She was able to work out of her home, be her own boss, and become successful at a young age of twenty-one. She and her husband were able to start their family. They were able to travel to many states and both became motivational speakers.

My Youngest Daughter

My youngest daughter is also a young woman with an average IQ. She was taking her college classes during her junior year of high school. She used and applied the "BASIC PRINCIPLE RULES OF

LIFE" and graduated high school in only three years at the top of her class as "MISS CUM LAUDE." She went on to achieve two: two-year college associates' degrees and one paramedic degree at the young age of only twenty-four.

My Son

My son is a twelve-year-old young man also with an average IQ. He wanted to join the band and learn to read music, so he could play the trumpet. His goal was to be good enough to reach the first chair.

Even at the young age of twelve, he was able to use and apply the "BASIC PRINCIPLE RULES OF LIFE" to accomplish this very goal during the second nine weeks of school. During the third nine weeks of school, he was beaten out of his first chair position. He did not give up, and again, he applied the "BASIC PRINCIPLE RULES OF LIFE" to accomplish his goal of being first chair. He indeed accomplished this goal during the last nine weeks of school. By using and applying the PRINCIPLES, my son was able to achieve his goal not once but two times in one school year.

Do your Home Work: Get a second opinion: Do your research: Compare your options: Do you have a plan?

Liberty Defined:
Fifty Essential Issues that
Affect Our Freedom

Congressmen and number one New York Times best-selling author Ron Paul returns with his most provocative, compelling arguments for personal freedom up to date.

The term "liberty" is so commonly used in our country that it has become a mere cliché. But do we know what it means, what it promises, and how it affects our daily lives? And most importantly, can we recognize tyranny when it is sold to us disguised in liberty's magnificent clothing?

Dr. Paul writes that "to truly believe in liberty is to divorce it from any desired social and economic outcome. To believe in liberty is to trust in the spontaneous actions and circumstances that emerge when the government does not intervene in human volition and cooperation. Liberty permits people to work out their problems for themselves, take risks, and accept responsibility for the results, and make their own decisions. It is the foundation of America."

Liberty Defined is a comprehensive guide to Dr. Paul's position on fifty of the most important and controversial issues of our times— from abortion to Zionism. Clear and fearless in its opinions, it sheds new light on a word that has been fast losing its rightful meaning.

Dr. Ron Paul is a physician and a twelve-term congressman from Texas who ran for president in 2008. He is the chairman of the domestic monetary policy subcommittee and the author of eight books, including the New York Times best sellers *The Revolution: A Manifesto* and *End the Fed*. An advocate of sound money, personal liberty, free markets, and international peace, he is chairman of the FREE Foundation, founder of the Campaign for Liberty, and distinguished counselor to the Ludwig von Mises Institute. He and Carol, his wife of fifty-three years, have five children, eighteen grandchildren, and three great-grandchildren.

The Survivor: Civilians Can Relate to a War Veteran's Experience

A current day issue can show how this works:

It is a beautiful day. As you say goodbye to your family before leaving to go to work, you suddenly realize just how much you enjoy their happy smiles and the exchange hugs and kisses with your wife and children! You also realize they are exactly what you live for, and they are the sole reason for your existence. You come home from a hard day's work and be greeted with smiles, hugs, and kisses from your family who have waited all day to get to see you once again. You shower, eat, and enjoy spending wonderful moments with your family before you go to bed only to wake up and do the same thing all over again. When you live for your kids, you live for the following experiences.

It is really a great feeling to sit on the side of your children's beds, telling them bedtime stories, pulling the covers up around them, and tucking them as they hold their arms up for one more hug and one more kiss as they tell you "I LOVE YOU, DAD!"

You respond saying, "I love you to the moon and back times infinity." You get up, turn out the light, and head into your own room where your lovely wife awaits. You crawl into bed next to your wife, set your alarm clock, turn out the lamp, and your wife and you exchange good-night hugs and kisses. You each say "I love you so much," and soon after, sleep claims you. Suddenly, in the middle of the night, the most HORRIFIC sound awakens you. You realize your house is going up in FLAMES. What are your first THOUGHTS? Do you save your family? Do you save yourself? Do you grab some personal materials? As these thoughts are raging through your mind, you only have mere seconds to decide what are you going to do and act. You choose to save your family. All of a sudden, you find yourself blinded by all the smoke and trapped by all the flames. Nonetheless, you search for your family as you hear their SCREAMS FOR HELP!

The firefighters arrive, and one helps you get out of the house. You thankfully discover that one other family member has made it outside unharmed. Then you see one firefighter after another carrying LIMP BODIES in their arms. You hear the most horrifying, blood-curdling screams of "OH MY GOD! NO! OH, PLEASE, GOD, *NO!*" These screams continue as you, with tears running down your face, realize it is your own voice screaming out at the top of your lungs to the same "OH MY GOD! NO! NO! OH, PLEASE, GOD, NO! THIS CAN'T BE HAPPENING!"

Now you have an idea what our service men and women who survived went through as they watched the most horrifying and heard the most blood-curdling screams from other men and women who were shot and were seriously wounded when an explosion went off, severing their legs and arms. This has happened and will continue to happen as service men and women continue to fight, so you and I can live in this great, free country, the United States of America. When you see someone who is displaying that they have served in the military, do you think you might show the courage and have the guts to ask them if anyone has told them thank you for your service to the United States of America? Will you have the courage and guts to shake their hand and say, "I personally would like to say thank you very much for your service and dedication to our country. I greatly appreciate what you stand for and all that you have been through for the USA, so my family and I can continue living a pampered life of freedom in this great country!"

Many of these men and women had a vision, a goal, and a purpose. They took that step to live their convictions of serving their country. They made decisions. Many of them as young adults. These are the choices you make in life. Step out of the "box." Others try to put you in plan. Think, educate yourself, set goals, and put a plan in motion to make yourself a success in life![1]

---

[1] (Grand Central Publishing New York & Boston: Hachette Book Group, Inc. First Edition: 2011)
Inside Front Flap and Inside Back Flap of Book Cover.

Proof that the Plan Works!

A uthor's note: The following stories are evidence that this plan works! These three men had doubts about themselves and what they could accomplish. They just set a goal and reached it. Imagine how their lives have changed because they sought out the Big Secret.

The next success story should be yours!

Do your Home Work: Get a second opinion: Do your research: Compare your options: Do you have a plan?

Plant Operator

One day at school, I walked and saw a classmate being bullied. As I watched the situation, I noticed that he was outnumbered, so I intervened. I yelled out, "Hey! One-on-one, okay?" I thought, *If that doesn't work, I will jump in and help the guy.*

One bully knocked books and papers out of the hands of the boy, and they all left. The poor kid looked at me in shock and confusion. I walked over, and he leaned down and picked up his things. I could see his papers with big grades written across them—100, 97, 95, 98, 99, and 100.

After we had gathered them together, he looked at me and asked why I had helped him. I told him I did not like the odds he was facing even though I felt it was not my business. Then he started to cry and sat down. I learned that his name was Chip, and I was sure anger and frustration were just a few of the emotions he felt.

When he spoke, he said something that expressed his frustration. "I am going to just quit because no matter how hard I try, people will always do whatever they can to stop me because I am black!"

Chip repeated with emotion, "I quit!"

I looked at him and replied "Now you are looking for sympathy, and you will find it between shit and suicide in the dictionary!" as I handed him his books and graded papers.

I assured him that if he quit now, he was stupid. "Let me tell you something that is from a country Boy Scout that you can use to shock everyone even yourself."

I then began to tell Chip how the school was giving out scholarships, "With the grades you have earned, just think how likely you are to get one! But you will never know unless you have the courage to try!"

The next time I saw Chip was at an assembly. At midyear, they were handing out scholarships, and there was only one person who was awarded—only one in the entire school! Yes, it was that young black student. The entire school was amazed and shocked. This young African American student was called to the stage and presented his award.

Do your Home Work: Get a second opinion: Do your research: Compare your options: Do you have a plan?

Ten Years Later

One of the men I worked with named Joey was a helper who was assigned to move pipes with an overhead crane. He would ask my opinion about past historical events. For example, he asked why Europeans wanted to wipe out the entire Indian race. He was consumed with a vendetta toward white people.

He had created a very thick large stonewall around himself. He also could not figure out what was keeping him from moving forward in life. As the hours and days went by and we worked together, I would answer Joey's questions based on the "Big Secret."

One day, after constantly hearing his complaint after complaint, I asked if he was looking for sympathy. He said, "Yes." I told him he could find it in the dictionary between shit and suicide.

"No matter what your race is, what happened in the past, it is over. It is water under the bridge," I told him. "Now you can learn from the past and use it constructively. But you cannot change it. You can only change what is front of you! You can make you or you can break you! Now quit your complaining. Get your butt in gear, and build yourself a plan and get moving!"

TEN YEARS LATER, Joey and I met at a different job location. We said hello, embraced, and I could see a happy look on his face. "Thank you, James! From the last time we worked together until now. I've joined the military, learned several skills, got my baccalaureate degree, and am a third level quality control inspector. I went from a low-paid employee to someone who is making close to $40 an hour!"

Do your Home Work: Get a second opinion: Do your research: Compare your options: Do you have a plan?

The $20 Bet

W hile employed as a pipe welder at a pipe fab shop, I had to deal with people who thought they were the elite in the whole company. Of course, there had to be rules and regulations, but this woman felt she could change the rules at any time. She also thought she could go back to the original rules whenever she wanted to. Sounds familiar?

After each safety meeting, everyone who worked on the floor would gripe and complain and point out the lack of common sense of this person in human resources who was supposedly in control. They felt this person was treating them like children or stuffed animals, which had been placed around a table and told when to do what and how to do it just like when they were children.

This woman felt so powerful she felt she could control everyone with her commands because she knew they would sit there and do nothing and take it. So I decided to use the Big Secret with these employees. I presented the issue to the woman from human resources in a professional, calm manner. The workers were pleased and satisfied with the outcome.

Throughout the course of time, I had often voiced my opinion toward people I worked with. They asked me how I would go about handling their issues, problems, and desire to achieve goals. My responses were always based on the Big Secret.

These people were skilled craftsmen: helpers, fitters, welders, foremen, and those in quality control. One day, a fellow worker, a pipefitter, came to my station asking how I figured out how to handle the major problems that we're all facing with the person in human resources.

I asked him why he wanted to know, and he said he had seen me use the skill several times and wanted to learn them. Again, I asked him why he wanted to know.

"I have an issue between the school and my son."

I told him I would teach him but figured he would probably laugh because it is so simple.

"Well, to be honest, I am a little scared," he said. "I dropped out of high school in the tenth grade, but I got my GED. But you know, I am a Mexican with no college education. I want to be able to do what you do."

I asked him, "Are you looking for sympathy because of your view of the past?"

"Well, yes. I guess I am," he responded with a chuckle. I told him that he would be fine.

"You will find sympathy in the dictionary between shit and suicide! Do you want to make a bet?"

He looked at me with a curious look on his face, and I just smiled.

"What do you mean 'bet'?" he asked. I told him I would bet my paycheck against his.

"If I show you several simple steps and you follow them completely, you will be very pleased with the outcome," I challenged him.

"You will be very pleased with the outcome in a professional manner resolving the issue you have with the school."

He began back pedaling with excuses! I told him, "The one person who will always stop you is YOU! Now you want to win and solve the issues, or do you want to take the coward's approach or lose from here on in your life?"

He looked at me with a bit of anger. I just smiled and said, "Well, what is it going to be?"

He said, "I don't want to bet my paycheck." So we agreed on $20, and I showed him the simple little steps I had learned myself.

I showed him how he could automatically orchestrate a plan. Now all he had to do was put it into motion and follow it out with persistence.

Close to a week went by before he spoke to me again, not even a hello or goodbye. One day, he walked over to me, put his hand in his pocket, pulled out something, and slid it under my clipboard. I raised a corner of the clipboard and saw $20.

I smiled and asked him how it all turned out. "I still don't believe it, but it was so simple. The school officials complimented me on being very professional. The issue was resolved, and everyone was satisfied.

"I did not think I could do it," he went on. "I did not think I could do it, but I did. I never would have guessed something so simple could have such a successful impact as this did." I asked him how he felt about himself and what his next goal would be.

He said, "If you would write a book, I would buy it!"

"Why?" I asked.

He answered, "Because I found that I can use this in any and all my issues in life. I can also teach my kids how to use it for their own successes."

Do your Home Work: Get a second opinion: Do your research: Compare your options: Do you have a plan?

A Problem…and Its Solution
(Shawn's Story)

My college professor just wasn't teaching me or any of the other students the materials we needed for our drafting class. We all had to learn the course work in order to pass the drafting class and get our degrees!

I paid $2,000 out of my own pocket for the three months of class because I wanted to move up in the workforce and have a better life. I knew that if this professor did not teach the materials we all needed, we would all end up spending another $2,000 to take the course again so that we could pass the exam, and that would also mean six months in school.

I was angry, worried, and frustrated. I really did not know what the solution would be to make the necessary changes. I was afraid my work would be affected as well because I was not focused, and that might result in an unsafe work environment. I was afraid I would lose my job because I could not concentrate on my work responsibilities because this had become such a big problem.

I shared my concerns about the time and money I might lose because of a teacher who simply was not teaching the course. I spoke to several people as I sought a solution and then met James. Because he was a college graduate and seemed to have some good ideas, I thought it wouldn't hurt to approach him.

I asked if he could give me some advice if I told him about my problem or tell me how he would handle it if it were his issue. I laughed at him not thinking he could really help me. James said he would give me some helpful hints under one condition: I had to be "coachable." I told him I would, still laughing at him wondering how he could think he knew more than me.

But because I had agreed to listen, James told me he would set up a plan for me to follow. Still not sure he really knew the solution, I gave him a little attitude. He said to me, "I thought you were coachable."

And I saw a look in his eyes that told me I best stop talking and start listening to what he had to say!

The Plan!

James gave me a list of questions that made me think and take action. Here's what he taught me:

1. Have faith in who you are, where you are going, where you came from, and how you represent.
2. To think outside the box, you must dismantle YOUR box for life.
3. When you run into an obstacle, stop and rethink your plan. There is another way!
4. When confronting an issue, do your homework and research, so you will be comfortable that you are standing on solid ground.
5. Learn the system, and more doors will open than you can ever imagine.
6. Do not be afraid of rejection.
7. Don't be afraid to address someone who has a higher working status. They are just as afraid of you.
8. Everyone has a boss!
9. The rewards can be astronomical. Simply show your appreciation, and always say thank you.
10. Now put the plan into motion one step at a time!

Do your Home Work: Get a second opinion: Do your research: Compare your options: Do you have a plan?

A Note from James

After Shawn came to me for help and finally decided to follow the above ten steps, he met with the dean. Using his usual humor yet expressing his concern over his professor, Shawn was able to get his message across. He was losing time, money, and, possibly, his future!

The dean took action assigning a substitute teacher to the course, and everyone in the class learned the material, passed the exams, and got their degrees. They ended up getting their money's worth.

Shawn, a proud African American, recently graduated and is continuing to work as a welder while seeking a job as a draftsman, wanting to advance in the workforce and earn a better income for his family.

To me, Shawn is a leader and hero because he was willing to find a solution to not only his problem but those of his classmates. He changed not only his life but those of the other students as well.

The Unawareness of How One Language Turned into Two Different Languages

Although most people would agree that men and women are different, just how different is still undefined for most people. Many books in the last ten years have forged ahead alternating to define these differences. A definitive guide is needed for understanding how healthy men are different from healthy women. There is a need to improve relations between the sexes. It is necessary to create an understanding of an understanding of our differences that raise self-esteem and personal dignity while inspiring mutual trust, personal responsibility, increase cooperation, and greater love.

I have been able to define posture terms of how men and women are different. As you explore these differences, you will feel walls of resentment and mistrust melting down. You will find yourself nodding while reading this book. Say, "Wow, wow, this is me you are talking about." You are definitely not alone because others have benefited from applying the insights of this book. You can as well.

This reveals how men and women differ in so many areas of their lives. Not only do men and women communicate differently, but they think, feel, perceive, react, respond, love, need, and appreciate differently. They almost seem to be from different planets, speaking different languages and needing different nourishment.

The results of this new program for understanding the opposite sex is not only dramatic and immediate but also long lasting. When you want your computer to have more knowledge, you add new program. Your brain is a computer. So here you are adding new information.

This new approach whereby your relationships can successfully support you in solving so many of life's problems as they arise. With this new awareness, you will have the tools you need to get the love, appreciation, and respect you deserve. Then give to your partner the love and support he or she deserves.

Yet repeatedly, I have heard people say that they have benefited more from this new understanding of relationships, and it creates great therapy and counseling for both parties.

"I wish someone had told me this before." It is never too late to increase your understanding and the love in your life. You only need to learn a new way. Whether you are in therapy or not, if you want to have more self-fulfillment and more fulfilling relationships with the opposite sex, this book is for you. May you always grow in wisdom and in love.

You and your children deserve a better means of enjoying life. Now ask yourself or others why you have not been told of this. Is it possible that this information was in schools? There is a question, why was it taken out? Who took it out of circulation? Why?

This is why our parents never knew and, therefore, could not have taught us what they did not know!

Do your Home Work: Get a second opinion: Do your research: Compare your options: Do you have a plan?

Let's Start at the Beginning

When you are first brought into this world at BIRTH, you are engulfed into the world of EMOTION because your parents flood you with love and joy! As you grow into a toddler, your loving mother wraps you up into her world of EMOTION. Your father holds you up with pride, love, and joy. As you grow to the elementary age, here, most parents have already started teaching common sense.

For example, they teach you to understand right from wrong. But COMMON SENSE is coated with EMOTION! Let's go back in time and look at this. If you are a son, when you started playing with your cars and trucks or blocks, here is where you started to think "LOGICALLY" because if you dropped your car or truck, did that hurt your feelings? The answer is NO. Did your car or truck were feeling hurt? The answer is NO.

As you learn to ride a bike and your dad is helping you, you remember how many times you and the bike fell down plus getting hurt. Dad said you will be okay. Just get up and try again because if your feelings got hurt or your pride, that is not going to teach you to learn how to ride a bike. ONLY PRACTICE! So you can see a young boy to a young man. You are dealing with physics. Here, you can see that you are starting to learn and master this "through process" and speaking the language of LOGIC.

If you are the daughter, let's go back in time to look at this. You are mirroring your fantastic loving mother! You watched her actions. Here, you want to be just like her. "That's great." So you have your dolls and/or stuffed animals to playhouse with. Remember how you used to talk to them as you dressed them pretending that they were your children? Here, you are also pretending to be the head of the household the same way you see your mother's actions with the family in the house.

Remember the days when you would talk and dress your dolls just like Mother would talk and dress you? Remember when you would put your doll in the little chairs as you set the little table? You would place cups and saucers in front of each doll just like the whole family sitting down to eat breakfast or dinner. Remember when you told your dolls to clean their plates and drink all their juice? Remember when your mother firmly told you the same thing plus eat all your mac n' cheese? Remember when you said very firmly to your dolls, "Don't just sit there. Eat all your mac n' cheese"? Then remember when you said "Don't talk back to me!" while all along, the dolls were just sitting there staring at you, motionless and not saying a word, showing you total control.

Now remember when you are starting elementary and high school you wondered if all the boys thought you were pretty? Do you remember having all your girlfriends around, and you would talk about all kinds of things based on how you felt toward each subject? Do you remember right after graduation how wonderful you felt because now you felt like you could fulfill a goal or a career and get married to a fantastic man, have children, and live happily ever after just like in the movies? From as far back as you can remember up to the age sixteen to eighteen years of age, what you may not realize is you have mastered the thinking and speaking the language of emotion with common sense. Congratulations! You have done a fantastic job! Here is the same thing you may definitely take the time to think about.

Do you feel anger, frustration, and even upset when talking to your partner as well as to others? The answer is yes. The other person maybe speaking the same language. Think about the environment you were raised in. Who raised you? What did you just read? Think about this. Subconsciously, are you talking or treating the person you are talking to like a stuffed animal or a doll setting at your play table? The reason I ask this question is because this has happened to me more than once. When having a conversation with a wonderful woman, it does not take very long for me to bring it to the attention of the woman. I am not passive and think and speak logic that I am not one of her dolls or stuffed animals.

I do this in a very nice, educational way by reminding her of when she was very young, mirroring her mother while playing with her dolls. I have found that when these occasions occur, the woman showed a ___ facial expression because to their credit, they are thinking about their past.

Then with a smile, she will say, "You know, I did not realize I was doing that." I would say that is okay because that is "what you learned during those years of your life."

Yes, everyone repeats that of what you have learned. It is interesting to hear the woman say they know they need to learn to use more logic. I would ask them if I may pay them compliment. She would say with a smile, "Yes, you can."

I would tell them, "I am impressed with admiration that you would like to learn and use additional logic in your life. You will find many rewards."

Do your Home Work: Get a second opinion: Do your research: Compare your options: Do you have a plan?

My Two Little Girls

I enjoy being very active participant in their lives. One day, while watching them playhouse with their dolls and stuffed animals, I noticed them talking to the dolls as if they were their children, getting their play table set up for a lunch or dinner and placing all their dolls in all the chairs. I could not help but notice they were talking to their dolls in almost the same tone and manner that their mother would talk to them at the table. Their mother, with a firm tone, tells them to clean their plate and drink all the juice.

One day, on a separate account, while watching and listening to the conversation my daughter was having with the dolls, I would step in the room and ask them if they ever think that the doll may be coming down with an illness or has filled up on junk food like snacks. Maybe that is why they are not hungry. Logically, that is why they are not cleaning their plate or drinking their juice. My girls would just look at me and say, "I did not think about that." With a compliment of kind gesture, I would remind them that they need to be open minded. They asked what that is.

You need to learn how to think and speak, but know the difference between emotion and logic so that when the time arises, you can have a fabulous conversation with whoever you are talking to. Their response was "I did not think about that." I did not know there were two different languages. I told them, "That's okay because I am going to teach you the difference between the two and how to master them both."

Over the years, I am very proud of them because of the outstanding goals they have accomplished. They have replied to me to say they have really seen the harmonious difference with their husbands, children, and associates. I am also very proud of them.

When we get together and visit, during our conversations, they are constantly saying "Dad, logically, this is how I accomplished this task." When they are talking to their mother, they are constantly pointing out to their mother that logical is a better way!

You are your child's mentor.
You must do this exercise.
Then practice it for the rest of your life.

Go to your study and get a dictionary. Then call your children for all of us to meet in at the kitchen table. After all is present, explain to them that you are going to teach them a course of home school about how to speak two different languages and how to think two different languages. Then explain that not too many people realize the difference of the two. Because of this, there are people while having a conversation, get upset, angry, frustrated, and create a lot of arguments. Now we are going to learn how to eliminate these problems before they get started.

Tell them, "The first thing is we are going to look up is the definition of words. We will be talking about their meaning. Then we will talk about examples so that you will fully understand the meaning of what you are about to learn. Now take your pen and paper and write down the definitions as we cover them."

o NONWILLING
   One who does not try.
o WILLING
   The power of mind to decide and do deliberate control over through an action.
o PASSIVE
   Receiving or subjected to an action without responding or initiating an action in return.
o NONPASSIVE
   Questing the subject on known facts.

o NON-AGGRESSIVE
  No desire for pursuing or persistence; evade trouble.
o AGGRESSIVE
  Inclined to move or act; persistence.
o OPEN-MINDED
  Having or showing a mind open to new arguments or ideas.
o COMMON SENSE
  Having or showing ordinary good sense: sensible and practical.
o USE YOUR IMAGINATION
  The ability to create new things or ideas or to combine old ones in to new forms.
o THINK OUTSIDE THE BOX
  To plan, discover or compose; denoted to thoroughly engage intellectual or theoretical working.
o EMOTION
  A strong feeling: fear, anger, love, joy, and grief.
o LOGIC
  Logic is not the science of belief but the science of proof or evidence.
o DECISIONS
  The deciding or setting of a question, dispute or an act; by giving judgment to one side.

Once you have done this with your children and, however, with your spouse, keep a very positive attitude because you can have so much fun with laughter. Think about this every day when you are with your family members. You are discussing something. In our lives, we have to be talking to someone. So this exercise is an everyday thing. Why, because we talk all the time? This is when you put this knowledge to work and use it! Think about it. When your kids come home from school or your spouse comes home from work, what is the question you must likely ask first? How was your day? What did you do today? How did everything go? Were there any problems?

Right here is where you will help your children prepare and your spouse will appreciate you even more. As each family member informs you of what happened that day and the decisions they made toward the situation, you ask them "Was it your decision to do what you did. Why?" Ask for a reason. Was it based on an emotional decision? Or was it based on logical decision? Give them time to answer the question because this is very important for them to learn this skill. Were you open-minded? Give them a chance to answer the question.

Did you use your common sense? Answer the question. Did you use your imagination? Answer the question. Did you think outside the box? Your children and spouse may look at you rather peculiar. They may say, "You know that is a good question." Here, you need to talk to them as a friend or mentor and show appraisal to them as you walk with them through the whole conversation so that the individual will see and understand their decisions that they made. This will help them to be better prepared to make the next decision that they will be facing with. You need to do this with your family every day. Your family members will "learn" to appreciate this knowledge by experiencing the results. You will appreciate the harmony in your family.

Teach your kids to do examples every day, until it becomes second nature.

THINK: about what you are going to say.

BEFORE: you say it!

"Logic" is based on facts.

Outside the rain is pouring down. When you start to say a sentence. The FIRST word is LOGICAL you will ruin, those brand new leather expensive shoes from walking in water.

"Emotion" is based on feelings.

You are fixing to go out into the public. So you apply hair products to your hair as you style it, and apply nice make up to your face. So you will feel very attractive.

Emotionally, you are going to get very upset, angry, frustrated, lose pride, and feel less attractive. When the wind and rain damages your hair style and make up.

Do your Home Work: Get a second opinion: Do your research: Compare your options: Do you have a plan?

Experience: Known to Be the
Best Means of Learning

When one is talking about a topic and has no experience and no learned history facts of proof in the matter, you will find that their comments are based on thinking and speaking the emotional language. I have some of the most fantastic relatives. In this story, I am going to talk about one of my aunts whom I don't get to see much of.

One day, we were visiting, and she was asking me about different things of my life. The conversation went on. Then she asked me what I thought about the Second Amendment. So I asked her if she could be more definitive. So she said, "I don't feel like we should have guns at all."

I asked her for more details. She replied, "I feel there is no need for anyone to have the right to have or carry a gun here in the United States." She continued to say, "Look at all those people who had been killed by guns like the people in the Colorado theater or that church and that night club! If no one have guns, this would not have happened. I feel fear when I go shopping or to the theater and the gym. This just makes me angry to think I could get shot or killed."

"Well, Aunt O, first thing, is a gun a tool? People kill people with whatever is convenient to them at the time."

Now I respect my aunt. I respect her feelings and point of view. I am a good listener. Before I said anything to respond to what my aunt said, first thing I did was with respectful humor. I first laughed. "Why?" Now stop and think about this like I did.

(1) What language is she thinking and speaking: emotion or logic? I noticed in my opinion she was thinking and speaking the language of emotion. Why? She used keywords of the definition of emotion. Here, I realized, and you can see this also.

I will be thinking and speaking the language of common sense and logic. So you and I already know of the problems that are fixing to happen because you have two people talking about the same topic but are thinking and speaking two different languages. Now as our conversation continued, I remained humorous because there was no need to getting mad or angry toward her.

At this point, I pointed out to her that we were going to have a major different opinion on the subject because she is basing her thought on emotion of how you feel. I based my opinion of proof and evidence. This is known to be LOGICAL COMMON SENSE. So here we were having a nice conversation while speaking two different languages.

For example: After World War II, there was a small country who passed a law to ban all firearms. Then a large a country walked right in the small country and announced, "Now your country belongs to us." The little country had no way to defend themselves from the invasion.

I reminded her, "Right now, you are living in a fantastic country. Compare it to the freedom of other countries including third-world countries just so you will learn to appreciate just what you have! Better yet, move and live in a different country so you can gain experience of the difference of what you call freedom."

People have warned us by movies that if we do away with the second amendment, a different country will come in and take the country over. Even the Japanese, after bombing Pearl Harbor, one admiral asked the emperor, "Now that we have bombed Pearl Harbor. Why don't we send in ground troops and take over the country?"

The emperor said that would be committing suicide. The admiral asked why.

The emperor said, "Because the US citizens are so heavily armed!" That is what has saved our country of the United States of America from being invaded—the second amendment. Even though we live in the twentieth century, we still have "survival" in our genes back to the cave-man days wherein if one group has food, the second group may ask the first group to share. But if the first group does not share, therefore, the second group will attack with force. This is called "survival."

First of all, I explained to her that this was my pastime hobby. Like so many other people who did the same thing, everyone who bought and used a metal detector had the adventures and possible thrill of finding something of value buried in the sand or dirt.

When I bought my first metal detector, I was thinking with EMOTION. Living in the twentieth century, I knew there were no claim jumpers nor back shooters. The chance of being robbed were slim to none also because we have all the laws of protection plus you only heard of someone else being robbed or killed. I, like so many people, thought I was invincible. It will never happen to me. Soon after the beginning of my treasure hunting adventures, I was being faced with some close calls of being robbed in broad daylight.

Now I managed to stand and hold my ground and not get robbed or possibly injured or killed over just a few coins not even enough to buy a Coke to drink. But to robbers, when they see someone on the "example," the beach with a metal detector, all they see in their mind is that person with the detector has already found a treasure. "A lot of money." They figure their robbery is going to be easy pickens. Sadly, I knew two very nice, good-hearted men whom I would socialize with on the beach while all of us would use our detectors to find coins buried in the sand that were both robbed of their finding and then killed in broad daylight.

With this reality, I needed to face common sense and logic. I had my gun permit but did not carry my gun with me onto the beach. Do you think I was stupid or smart at this point? Do you think I was thinking EMOTIONAL or LOGICAL? One day, during broad daylight, I was minding my own business having a blast in what I was finding in the shallow water there on the beach. I am not going into details. First I thank the good Lord above—"GOD." Second my means of standing and holding my ground. I came so close to getting robbed then shot! I was staring my death in the face.

The CEO of the NRA has a saying, "How do you stop or neutralize a bad person with a gun? With a good person with a gun!"

As I continued to talk to my aunt, I told her she was speaking the language of emotion. Now what I just covered was history. "Now I respect your opinion. But it is quite clear you have no history, knowledge, or experience. That is the number one teacher. This is the number one problem with people here in the United States of America—lack of common sense, lack of logic, and the lack of experience."

She replied, "So do you have experience?"

I told her of an incident that happened.

*****

Experience is the best teacher. Learned the hard way.

One day, we were on the beach. I was playing with my metal detector. It was fun to find coins buried in the sand. I learned a long time ago that you are not invincible nor thinking this will happen to you. Thinking this kind of things only happen to someone else was the biggest problem with people. You think and feel that nothing will ever happen to you! That you are invincible. Guess what, you are not!

While on the beach, my son, ten years old, was building a sandcastle while I was close by using my metal detector. I had schooled my son to watch for other people on the beach so that he could learn what to watch for danger because when you had seen the real thing, figure of speech, he will always know what to look for.

All of a sudden, my son says, "Dad, Dad! Look there are three men heading right to us."

So I asked my son, "So do they look mean? Are they in a hurry? Are they mad looking? Do they have a friendly smile on their faces?"

My son said, "Dad, turn around and look!" I asked how far away they were from us. "I don't know!"

"Are they from the house to the stop sign?"

"No, Dad, they are closer."

"When they get from the mailbox to the house, let me know."

Example, teaching him how to ___ distance.

Quietly, he said, "Dad, Dad, they're here." Due to the past experience, I have learned to carry a firearm in public places in good daylight. You will see why!

As the three men were approaching, all along, I had my back to them with my right hand under my left armpit and with my gun in hand and finger on the trigger. Example, I was using my son's eyes to see with!

"Dad," my son said with a low voice. I turned around with my hand on my gun, ready to draw if I had to! "Hello, fellows. How are you doing?" They lifted their shirts to show me their guns that were tucked in their pants. There, for a few seconds, the three men did not move or say a word.

All of a sudden, one was slowly moving his hand toward his gun. "You must be the most stupid of the three because you need to recalculate this situation. Beating on who can pull their weapon first and fire because I guarantee you, I will beat you. That includes the other two."

All of a sudden, one of three did speak in a hurry "Bob, don't be a fool and get me shot" as we all stand there in suspense to see if guns were going to be drawn. Then the same guy that spoke to Bob said, "Is that your son?"

"Yes, he is. We're just out having a son and dad day."

"Well, you and your son have a great day."

"Why, you fellows do the same."

They walked away. So I asked my son after it was all over, "Why did no one have to pull their gun?"

"Because, Dad, when they realized that you had a gun, then things became balance. They did not want to get shot."

"Yes, you are correct. The number one fear is no one wants to get shot! People think that back in the Western day, there was the only time of claim jumpers, back shooters, and robbers. They are ___. Because it still goes on today!"

Do your Home Work: Get a second opinion: Do your research: Compare your options: Do you have a plan?

The Woman I So Highly Respect with Admiration

While being unemployed, on a particular date, you need to report to an address which is the location of a workforce center to possibly find what is available for employment in your field. Once you get to enter the building, you notice people in small booths looking at computer screens. Now this is your first time to attend such a location. First thing you realize is that your job does not consist of using a computer. You are a pipe welder. So feeling a little out of place, you see this very nice-looking woman standing up from her desk saying, "Just a minute, and I will assist you."

A couple minutes later, with a pretty smile and handshake, she invites you into her office area. "Have a seat." You notice early in her introduction and the following questions to be very professional. She asks you about your background and life, in general. The manner in which she use is very impressive. But why are you impressed? Because she is using keywords of logic. You are waiting to hear keywords of emotion. But there are none. Your conversation continue into your personal life. You suddenly look at her thinking, *Wow, she would be a fantastic business partner because of the language she is speaking.* You then ask her if it would be all right with her if you could pay her a compliment.

"Why, of course you can."

You reply as she holds on interesting posture and smile, "I would like to compliment you on the language you are thinking and speaking."

With a smile on her face and sparkle in her eyes, she replies, "Thank you."

"It is really nice to speak to a woman who is very unique in their own way."

With a very large smile, blushing facial appearance, and sweet, sparkling eyes, she replies, "Thank you. That was very nice of you. But what do you mean? You are speaking with logic and logical common sense. With a straightforward facial expression."

She says something you are totally unprepared to hear. It took me four marriages to finally learn that! Consciously, is there a man now who is ___ with a fantastic woman that is very unique in her own way and a great business partner? Because now she knows when to speak the same language when needed and also has learned the difference of the emotion and logic. She just smiles with pride showing self-esteem.

"Yes, there is a wonderful man in my life again. It is amazing how well we get along. The trouble I have with my previous husbands just melt away. Arguments."

"Can I pay you another compliment?"

With sparkling eyes and blushing smile, she replies, "Sure, you can."

"I admire you with admiration."

Again, with a blush facial expression, pretty smile, and sparkling eyes, she replies, "Thank you. But why?"

"You are the first woman I have ever met that has showed the guts and courage to admit the value of learning the difference of the two languages. Then speaking the correct language when needed."

You notice her blushing red face and her soft smile as she is collecting moisture in both eyes using tissues and softly said, "Thank you. I have just one question."

"By all means, ask."

"When two people get together and help each other in a unique way as we have done here then both of you sense a friendly, soft, warm hug in the air around them. My question is, do they pass and leave everything in question, or do they share the hugs and make a full circle in means of showing their appreciation and respect to the other?" she asks with her loving facial expression and watery eyes.

"Yes, I would take and share the hugs to show my appreciation." You move slowly toward her. You gently come into contact with her body. Your heart is racing. You can feel your blood pressure, and your body temperature is raising fast. You gently wrap your arms around her as she slowly wraps her arms around you. You slowly move one hand up between her hair and neck as you gently massage her neck while the other hand slowly moves to her lower back. She squeezes you more firmly. You notice the aroma of white diamonds to intensify. The enhancement of seconds seems like minutes. You both release tension in your arms. She looks at you with a passionate, loving smile as she gives you a kiss on the cheek. You can see the heat waves.

"Thank you for the hug."

"You're welcome. Goodbye. Take care of yourself."

"She is a role model."

Your Mom and Dad,
My Moms and Dads

L ike you, I have a mother and father. But in my early years, while my mom and dad were at work, they would take my brother and me over to my aunt and uncle's house, so she could watch us. It is a long story, but my aunt and uncle became our stepmom and stepdad.

Let me point out. I respect both dads equally and both moms equally. Now my aunt and uncle took on the role as parents while my parents were away. You know you have two grandfathers and two grandmothers, so why not two moms and dads? Now both set of parents were loving, caring, and obedient. I learned a great deal from both. At the same time, I learned to master logical common sense from my stepparents. The stepparents raised eight kids. They took the time to educate all of us kids to understand the difference of making a decision, a decision based on emotion, and a decision based on logical common sense. They taught us that logical common sense has the highest reward in accomplishing whatever decision toward accomplishing a goal. All eight of us kids can look back on all our goals we had set and accomplished. We have all said we all have so much. Thanks to her (stepmom) and our stepdad. It is very hard to just put into words and hold the tears of appreciation. How much we all admired her and miss her teaching. One of the most fantastic admired lady.

Becoming Your Child's Best Friend

Pick a day when everyone is having or has had a good day. Ask your son or daughter to sit down with you, so the two of you can have a conversation. Ask your son or daughter for their opinion and maybe some advice or feedback on certain topics. Their response is typically "okay" or "yes, sir" because now you are getting older, smarter, and sharper. Make a point to tell them you are really proud of them for their achievements in life. Ask them to help you with certain issues or topics. Now you'll notice their facial expression is one of delight. You might also notice they may seem a little surprised because you have addressed them with admiration, respect, dignity, and as an independent individual.

Now let's take a few minutes to see if you can help me view things from different angles. Keep in mind that your son or daughter will show suspense in their facial expression. Really enjoy their expression because you will always remember this moment as a possible "Kodak" moment because you are asking them for assistance "HELP" with respect.

I'd also like to point out that in saying certain words or phrases, your tone of voice can have a good effect. But the other side is, this can also have a very bad effect on the person you are talking to. Think about what you are going to say before you describe or say it.

For example, if you or I say "You dumb stupid, kid. You made a big, bad stupid mistake based on your dumb decision" with sarcasm, how do you think your child is going to react? Real, easy answer. Remember how you reacted when this happened to you? This is what I am going to say. You were faced with making a decision in a very unexpected manner where you did not have or take the time to think it through because it took you by surprise. Therefore, the decision you made has put you in the situation you are in or facing.

Are you ready to begin?

The look on their face of sincerity. Yes, sir. Yes, ma'am.

Okay, I am going to start with this. I am your parent, okay?

With a blank look, they reply, "Yes, sir."

As a parent, my job consists of many responsibilities. "I love you. You are my child no matter how old you are. Therefore, I am going to protect you from different elements you will be facing as you go through life. My job is to teach you right from wrong. Guide you in the best way I know, coach you the best I know, and give you advice from what I have learned in life. It is very important to let you know that when you are wrong, there are consequences, and I have to enforce those consequences. Now sometimes the consequences may be very severe. I do not do this to hurt you mentally or physically. To tell you a little secret, it hurts me more than you know." You'll see your child's facial expression turn to surprise. "They had no idea."

"I choose to do this because I love you and care for you. You learn things best through experience. Now I know that this has caused you to fear me. Right?"

With a slow low tone of voice and eyes looking down at the floor, he says "Yes, sir."

"I know that there are times when you would like to talk to me about different things or issues you have faced from time to time, right?" An interesting look on his face.

"Yes, sir."

"That is okay. Because now I understand." You see their eyes lighten up. "Now you and I know because of the past, you have developed a 'fear.' You figure that you will be scolded and most likely be reprimanded or punished." You can see the answer of yes written all over their face. Yes, they are scared of you!

"Therefore, I am not the number one person you want to discuss any issues with." You see in their facial expression how they very much agree with you.

"One day when you become a parent, you will have a better understanding of where I am coming from."

"Okay, yes, sir."

"I am asking you to give me a chance to eliminate your fear to talk to me."

"Okay, yes, sir," he replies with a "WOW" look on his face.

"I would like to point out to you due to your age and mentality, you see, I know that when you have a serious issue to face, and you deal with it like so many other people. Guess what? Even myself when I was your age. You and I would rather go and discuss the issue with our best friends before you will discuss it with your parents. Why? Because you had no fear of your friend. Am I right so far?"

With an impressed facial expression, he replies, "Yes, sir."

"Keep in mind it is nice to have friends to talk to. Sometimes they may give you good advice. Now due to the lack of experience and facts of life, their advice could send you down a bad road. This could become more dangerous."

Opinion—a formal judgment by an expert or a professional advice.

Suggest a carefully thought-out conclusion "based on facts" but without the certainty of knowledge. Getting a second opinion is always the most logical thing to do. Now you can compare which road is the best road to follow.

"So what do you think so far?"

With a very happy, impressed look on his face, he replies, "Dad, you have a very good point."

"Son, you will have to make decisions all through life. So are you going to base your decisions on emotion or logic?"

You notice his facial expression, the slight reddish pink color in his face, and the small amount of moisture building up in his eyes.

This occurs because of the time and effort you put forth to help them plus because of the love, respect, courage, and admiration they have for you. And also, the love, respect, courage, and admiration that you are showing them.

Now you are trying to not show the extra moisture in your eyes as you continue.

"You and I both want to keep an open mind. When you have something important or not, I would like to ask you to view me as a best friend." Pause. Give him time to process this information. "Not as a parent you fear to talk to." Okay. You notice a warm, happy, and delightful look on their face. Pause.

"Yes, sir."

"As a parent, I am not going to yell or scold you, okay?"

"Yes, sir."

"I will point out. By getting you to "think" about the circumstances that are present and that you are to deal with, I will go about this by asking you questions then making suggestions. So that you can make a very good logical approach on how you are going to resolve the matter."

"Okay. Yes, sir."

"I am going to show you courage, respect, and dignity as an independent individual going down the road of life. We are not perfect; we all make mistakes. You and I know we need to learn from our mistakes. So we do not make the same mistakes twice. I would like you to view me as your guide, advisor, mentor, and best friend. So what do you think?"

As you look at them, you see the reddish pink color in their face, moisture collecting in their eyes due to sincerity of their love and admiration to you.

You get up, walk over to them, and give them a hug. As you share this moment, you tell them how much you love them and how proud you are of them as you try to hold the moisture that is building up in your eyes.

"Do you think you can do this?"

A confident voice replies, "Yes, sir."

Wiping his eyes, he said, "You may be wiping your eyes, Dad."

"Yes. Thank you."

"You're welcome and thank you."

You will find in time how much of a stronger bond you will share with your child.

Do your Home Work: Get a second opinion: Do your research: Compare your options: Do you have a plan?

The Swim Meet

A high school student joins the school swim team. He has the outlook or the goal to be an excellent athlete with his sights on swimming faster than his classmates' swim time that are posted on the billboard that is displayed on the wall of the building that enclosed the pool. The new student is advised by a high-ranking member of the swim team to eat a light lunch. Here, the student eats breakfast, goes to school, then eats a light lunch which he is advised. At the last hour of school, he is to report to the gym where the pool is located to start class.

During class, he and the rest of his classmates are instructed by the coach to swim one hundred yards of freestyle then one hundred yards of breaststroke, one hundred yards of backstroke, and then one hundred yards of butterfly. To swim one hundred yards, that means he must swim the length of the pool four times.

Each day, he tries so hard. He pushes himself to the maximum with determination to beat the recorded times records on the billboard.

Each day after practice, he is very frustrated and tired. Then when he gets home, he does not feel like doing any homework. After several weeks of practice, the team is informed. On this date, they will attend their first swim meet. They will be racing against other students from a different school. He is excited, nervous, and wants to make his parents proud. He reminds himself, "I must swim faster than my opponents and win the race plus set a new record of a faster time than is posted on the billboard."

Once again, they are advised to just eat a light lunch and nothing else before the swim meet. The theory is for you to be lighter.

Then you can swim faster. He is in suspense and anxious about the swim meet knowing his parents are going to be there to support him. Five o'clock in the afternoon, the swim meet is getting started. The students are all suited up. They are ready and are waiting for their names to be called to compete in a race against students from a different school. He sits in the bleachers with his parents. The parents show and speak of encouragement. Suddenly to his startled surprise, his name is called over the loudspeaker. With delight on the parents' faces, they encourage him to do his best. "You can do it." The look on his face is one of nervous, scared, and proud.

"Thanks, Mom. Thanks, Dad." He leaves and reports to his assigned starting platform. All five students step up onto their platforms and get into their starting positions. *BANG!* The starting gun goes off. All five of the students dive into the pool then start racing against one another. His heart is pounding and his arms and legs are kicking and pulling as he races blindly to the other end of the pool where he has to turn around and swim the length of the pool three more times. He is pushing himself so hard while trying to see who is behind as well as who is in the lead. Finally, he is on the last lap of four. He touches the wall as a manner of finishing the race. As he stands there in the pool watching as his parents clap and cheer on him, he is waiting to hear the results of the race. Then the announcement comes through. He did not win the race. He placed third. He is devastated.

Getting out of the pool, he goes over to sit down with his parents.

"Son, that was a great job you did."

"Hey, you tried. You gave it your best. Even though you did not win this race, there will be others that you can try again to win."

With a disappointed look on his face, he smiles. "Thanks, Mom. Thanks, Dad."

"Son, we are very proud of you."

But to him, this was disgraceful to himself because he did not even come close to beating any time that was on record for the fastest time let alone win the race against four other swimmers. After the swim meet is over, everyone goes home. After returning home, the parents, one at a time, place their arms around their son kindly telling him, "You know what?"

"What, Mom? What, Dad?"

"We are your parents, but we would also like to be your best friend, advisor, mentor, and coach. So if you want to talk about something or you hear something that bothers you, maybe you have something on your chest you would like to get off, give us a chance, and talk to us. You may be surprised."

The look on his face was priceless. They exchange hugs.

"Thanks, Mom. Thanks, Dad."

"You're welcome."

A couple of weeks go by plus another swim meet with the same devastating results. The son is thinking over what his parents offered. He is thinking, *Yes, they are my parents. Why don't me, myself, and I give them the chance they asked for? They may be the coolest parents I could ever have.*

One day after practice, he addresses his mother, "Mom, you were in athletics in high school, right?"

"Yes, I was."

"Can you advise me of something I need to do or change to increase my speed and win a race?"

His mother, with raise eyebrows and sparkling eyes and a huge smile, said, "Try talking to your dad first."

There is surprised look he had on his face. "Remember, your dad was on the swim team when he was in high school. His name used to be on that billboard."

With a grateful emotional look of pride on his face, he replies, "Thanks, Mom."

His mother steps forward and wraps her arms around him.

"Give your dad a chance."

"Thanks, Mom."

"Your dad is on the patio grilling lunch."

He looks at his mom and takes a deep breath.

Okay, I can do this. And I need to take him a large glass of tea. With the glass of tea in hand, he walks out to the patio.

"Hey, Dad, would you like some tea?"

"Thanks, son. I believe I do."

"Dad, can we talk for a few minutes?"

"Sure, son. What's on your mind?"

"Dad, I want to do what you did when you were on the swim team when you were in high school. You got your name posted on the billboard for the fastest time."

"Okay, son, keep talking. I am just going to be a good listener."

"Dad, will you help me understand what I am doing wrong?"

Dad lays down the grill tongs, takes a large drink of tea, walks over to his son, places his arms around his shoulders, and looks at his son while shaking his head with a smile.

"Son, you are not doing anything wrong."

You see the emotion of concern in his face of the unknown.

"Then why can I not win a race? Or better my own race time?"

"Okay, son. Do you have a plan? Which to accomplish these goals?"

He replies with a blank look on his face.

"Okay, son. I will explain. By the way, I do appreciate you giving me a chance. Now are you ready to pay attention and observe with logic as a student?"

"Yes, sir."

"Okay, my advice is very simple. One, do these exercises at home. This will strengthen the main muscles that you are using during swimming. Two, eat a good meal one hour before the swim meet starts. You have to have fuel to burn to get 100 percent return. Remember logically it is always best to get a second opinion, okay?"

"Yes, sir. Thanks, Dad."

"You're welcome."

They shared a bonding hug.

"Just do this, then compare the difference. That's my advice. Then you decide which is the best advice to follow."

He takes his dad's advice. Two weeks until the next swim meet, he sets a new time record for himself and won the race.

Do your Home Work: Get a second opinion: Do your research: Compare your options: Do you have a plan?

A Family Relatives:
My Cousin
Earning the Red Badge of Courage

During our early years, we got to spend a lot of time together. So she was used to me asking her. "The decisions you made, was it based on emotion or logic?" Now it did not take long before she could speak language of logic very fluently because I would ask her "The decision you are fixing to make, is it—"

Before I could finish the question, she would give a very good thought out of process that her decision is based on logic. As the years passed, the families moved apart. Then I learned she got into barrel racing.

One day, out of the blue, her mother "my aunt" called me then asked me in a cracking, paused way (you can tell when you have received a phone call from someone who is extremely upset and trying to talk to you as they are trying to hold back and control their tears). She said in a very emotional way, "I need you to come up and visit."

"Sure, what's up?" You could tell by her voice she was calming down.

"I need you here right now!"

"Okay, I will tell you when you get here. Sure. I am on my way."

You hear her tears splashing as they hit the phone. "Just calm down. I am on my way."

"Thanks, babe. Bye."

It was early morning, so I dropped what I was doing because logically, that was way out of an ordinary phone call. How was it I just happen to go in the house for a drink? I passed the phone, and it rang. That sounded like something dangerous—maybe extremely dangerous situation that was going to happen but had not happened yet!

Now this is your relatives that you are going to help. Help what? You have a two-hour drive ahead of you. This will give you time to try to hold your emotions. Don't get a speeding ticket because you are in a hurry to get there. Don't get in an accident. Plus don't be a nervous wreck. If a police officer was to pull you over for speeding, just imagine how you would stutter or stumble over your words. This would only make things worse between you and the officer. You need to focus on logic and stay calm as if this is just a social visit like a party gathering.

Now you arrive at their house. As you get out of your truck, you see your aunt standing in the driveway next to her truck. You walk up to her as she is walking toward you. You can't help but notice her face is as red as a rose. Her eyes are flooded with tears. She is trying so hard to keep a straight face from going into hysteria. You open your arms. She covers her face with her hands to hide her extremely upset, emotional facial expression. As you wrap your arms around her for her to know comfort and security, she wraps her arms around you.

As she starts to break down, her body starts shaking as her tears roll from her eyes. You listen to the horrid roaring cry of emotion.

"Oh please, God."

You are just standing there holding her up as your eyes fill with tears.

"Let it go, then tell me what is going on."

Once again, you listen to the horrid sound of an emotional cry.

"Oh my God please."

You have no idea what is going on. A few moments passed. She calms down as you try to comfort her. Then with an extremely large hug from her. "I am all right. Thank you for coming in such a short notice."

You're standing there sharing the hug, trying to wipe the tears out of your eyes.

"You're welcome. Now I am in suspense. This is almost like a thriller. But I would really like some details of what is going on." She just looks at you with a smile.

"Come on in the house. Let's eat. You will be sleeping on the couch in the living room. We will discuss it tomorrow."

The night is coming to a close. Your cousin is still out with her friends. So everyone else is turning in for the night. About midnight, you wake up because you hear the front door open very slowly that is right in front of you fifteen feet away. You notice it is your cousin.

"Oh, hey. What are you doing here? I am going to watch you ride your horse and race barrels tomorrow."

"Hey, that's great!" We share a hug.

"Well, we need to go to sleep."

"Yeah, see you tomorrow." She goes to her room down the hall.

"Now you try to go back to sleep."

"Yeah, right." You are still in suspense from what your aunt has not told you. You are in a different house from your own. Needless to say, you are having trouble going back to sleep. You look at your watch—it is 2:00 a.m. All of a sudden, you hear noise coming from the front door. Your heart is pounding. You know when you are trying to get the key into the lock. That's the sound it makes. Then you notice the doorknob turning slightly back and forth. Your heart is pounding so hard that's all you can hear. You're trying not to panic. Things are happening so fast you don't even think to put on your pants.

You're asking yourself, *What should I do? Who is trying to get that door open at two in the morning? Is it a robber? Are we going to get killed?* Everything is happening so fast. You start to go alert your aunt and uncle when you notice the door opening very slowly. You have no form of a weapon. You ease quickly behind the door as the person comes into the house. You lunge forward quickly. Then you restrain them. Due to the commotion, the lights come on. There stands your aunt and uncle holding his weapon. Your cousin has her mouth wide open, and her eyes the size of a five-cent piece. They are looking at me barely dressed, holding a young man in a restraint only to find out it was one of my cousin's boyfriend.

You let him go from the restraint. He is told very boldly by my uncle to go home. He is lucky that he did not get fatally injured.

After the big commotion is over, you ask yourself, *Is this why I am here?* You look over at your aunt. You see her with a glow of pride and admiration on her face with this huge smile. You put your hands forward and ask, "Is this it?"

She walks over to you, gives you a great big hug, and whispers in your ear, "Thank you for what you have done. The big one is tomorrow, babe. Good night."

I don't think I am going to get any sleep tonight. Soon it is an early morning sunrise. Everyone gets up to eat breakfast. Your cousin comes in the kitchen with open arms, and you share a large hug together.

As she looks at you with a big smile and sparkling eyes, she says, "I really appreciate you coming all this way to watch me ride my horse and race barrels."

"You're welcome. I would not miss the opportunity and good luck."

"Thanks."

"You're welcome."

You turn to your aunt. "How do you want your eggs cooked?"

You notice her face slightly red as the tears flood her eyes.

"Scrambled will be fine."

Everyone eats. Time passes. Then it is time to load the horse into the horse trailer. Then everyone in the truck heads off to the Rodeo Grounds. Your aunt is driving with very little to say. You are in the passenger seat noticing her soak up her tears with a soaked napkin. So you try to act like nothing is wrong. So you spend the time visiting with your cousin in the backseat. This only lasts for a few minutes because you notice that your cousin is noticing the facial expression of her mother as she watches her mother dry her tears. You notice the facial expression now on your cousin's face of great worries and concerns with a light flood of tears in her eyes.

"Is my mom okay? What is going on?"

"There is just a little issue your mom and I are going to talk about. It is nothing, really. Just focus on all the logical things you need to be thinking about in order to get the best time in the race. It's okay. Trust me."

You notice your aunt's facial expression calming down. She tries to laugh.

"I hope you're right."

Your thought is, *I hope so too.* You take a big swallow because you still do not know how big the problem is. Finally everyone arrives at the Rodeo Grounds. Your aunt helps her daughter get registered and get set up to be ready to compete when her name is called.

During this time, again, the daughter, with a very serious look of concern as her face is turning emotionally red, asks her mother, "Mom, what is wrong? What is the matter?"

Now you see two women with tears in their eyes.

The mother, as she wipes her tears, says, "Don't worry about it. I will tell you later. Just go, and do your best." Your cousin, with tears in her eyes, looks at you with confusion and concern.

"What your mother will tell you is emotion later. Right now, you have to think logical in order to do your best. Make the best time at racing those barrels in this arena. So go and do your best with the thought of logic only! Go!"

Now the mother tells her daughter, "After you race, do not get off your horse. You are to stay on your horse and ride him over to the horse trailer. Do not get off your horse under any circumstances or unless I tell you it is okay." Now your cousin is not sure on how to take this. The mother says "Do you understand?" in a very firm tone of voice.

"Yes, ma'am."

Your cousin's name is called. You stand by the fence to watch. She does a fantastic job in handling her horse as the horse goes around each barrel at a fast speed without knocking over any barrels. Then they post her time. She takes the lead with the fastest time. Now with this time of excitement you are experiencing for your cousin, it is temporary relief of the suspense of what is possibly going to happen that has not happened yet of what you have not been told. As you watch your cousin ride her horse back over to the horse trailer, you enjoy seeing great pride with huge smiles on everyone's face.

"Congratulations, cousin."

"Thank you, cousin."

You enjoy seeing a sign of relief on the face of your aunt. All of a sudden, tears just start flowing from her eyes as she tries to hide her face. You reach over to comfort her. This turns into a very tight hug with more tears and break-down crying to follow. Your cousin sees this. She is in tears.

"Cous, I got this. Stay over there by the horse. Do not move okay?"

With tears in her eyes trying to understand, she replies "Okay, cous" with your aunt in your arms.

"Go ahead. Let the tension release."

You stand there holding her with your arms as you feel her body began to shake as she just cries. You let a few moments that feel like minutes go by, feeling her calming down.

"Now will you tell me what is going on? Because I am in a great deal of suspense. Plus I am having a hard time holding back the extreme amount of moisture that is building up in my eyes called tears!"

Your aunt calms down wiping her tears away while you are drying your eyes because you really don't want anyone to see your tears because you are the strong one.

"I don't want you and I and the family to have to attend to my daughter's, your cousin's, funeral. Your cousin had a boyfriend. They are no longer together. The boy will not let go. His attitude is, if he cannot have her, then no one can have her. He is going to seriously hurt her or worse! This is something you were shown ahead of time. Yes, it is horrifying."

"So you brought me with you to the Rodeo Grounds. Logically, that means the ex-boyfriend is here also."

"Yes." She pointed him out. "You turn and look in the direction and see three guys."

You notice she is still wiping her tears away.

"Can you please help us?"

"Who are the other two guys standing next to the one you pointed out?"

"They are his friends. They are going to help him carry out whatever he is going to do to my daughter." Her face just deepens to the color of red with the tears just pouring from her eyes. Again, you hold her in your arms for comfort and security as she tries to apply self-control.

Well, my dear, I will do something, but I am not sure what's the best move to do first! So I will give it some thought! First, you have to practice what you teach! Rule out emotion. Think with logic.

1. You could report this to the police. The policemen are great people. Any problem, they can do some good, but generally, they are faced with after something has happened.
2. There are three of them and one of you, "no good." If you get into a fight with them, you are looking at physical body injuries: "yours." And then end up in jail due to the starting of the fight. They would all testify as one. Three to one, "no good."
3. If you will talk to them as a person looking to pick someone up like a blind date, then maybe they will spill the intention or plan out when they are most likely to attack or subdue your cousin. So thinking logical, you choose number three.

Now you put your plan into action. You go over and start talking to them as a new friend in the area looking for somewhat action with a local girl. They have no idea you are related to the girl they were going to deal with. Through the conversation, they did spill out their plan, which was very disturbing due to ___ when and where they were going to attack. Now you have to decide what is the most logical decision to make.

1. You could notify the police, but generally, the police will tell you they cannot do much until after something has happened.
2. If the police are notified and the boyfriend is confronted by the police, then the ex-boyfriend is made even madder. He will get a second chance to attack.

3. Reviewing previous cases. This could become fatal for your cousin.
4. You have learned a lot of self-defense techniques over the years due to dealing with bullies in your years of school.
5. Logically, you know you cannot be with your cousin 24/7.
6. Teach your cousin your self-defense tactics that she can keep for the rest of her long life.

On the way to your aunt's house, your aunt is asking you, "Are you going to be able to help my daughter?"

"I will tell you when we get to your house!"

"I need to know now! It can't wait."

We finally arrive at the house from the Rodeo. Your aunt is very eager to listen to what you have to say after pulling up in the driveway and getting out of the truck.

"We need to stay outside and talk." She looks at you with suspense.

"Okay."

"Now I am going to stay the night because tomorrow, I am going to have to give my cousin a crash course in self-defense with your permission. I will need the help of her brother. This is going to take some hours. So when we do this, you tell your daughter to wear some old clothes that can get dirty and torn because this is no time to play. This is going to be the real McCoy!"

Your aunt just looks at you. You got it all. All through the night, your cousin and her brother and even your aunt would ask you what was going to happen tomorrow.

"You will find out tomorrow."

The next day, everyone gets up and eats breakfast. You tell everyone, "We need to go outside to the front yard." We are all standing in the front porch. You remind your cousin about the problem with her ex-boyfriend.

"I know that it has been set in motion to where he is going to rape and possibly kill you. Do you understand? This is no joke! This is real."

You notice you are talking to her like a drill sergeant. With tears forming in her eyes, she says, "I understand."

"Right now, the odds are not in your favor. But you are going to let me change the odds by what am I going to teach you. You have to be serious. Thinking logic!"

"Okay."

"You tell your aunt I need you here throughout the whole session."

"Okay, you got it because I have to have your permission to show and teach. There is going to be some things you may not like. But it is necessary. It can be the difference of life or death."

Your aunt looks at you with a scared facial expression.

"Okay, you got it."

Now you explain to the brother how he is going to help you train his sister. "This training is very serious. So you have to act like you are serious. Is this whole matter understood?" He nods. "I did not hear you. Is this whole matter understood?" You say with a loud stun voice.

"Yes, sir!"

Then you talk to your cousin. You tell her, "I am very proud of you because you have shown to be thinking with a lot of logic throughout the years. Now is the time once again. You have to think with pure logic."

"Yes, you can count on it."

You tell her that this crash course is no joke. "You have to stay focused if you want to live because otherwise, we will be attending your funeral, or you will be so scared up physically and mentally. You won't even get a chance to live your life out right. Now you are going to see me and your brother as a different person. So when we go through this, in your mind, we are your attackers only. Do not make the emotional mistake. I am your loving cousin."

"Yes, sir."

You walk around the yard picking up large long sticks and short small twigs. You explained to her that these are to represent their bones and that she is going to learn to break them plus vital body pressure points because there are three of them and only one of her

"You have to be able to take them out of commission one by one as fast as you can. In 'street fighting, there are no rules.' You will learn how to defend yourself even if you are on your back. You will learn to break bones. Don't focus on trying to keep your clothes from being ripped off. You will have to forget about modesty because if you don't learn this, you will get raped and most likely killed from a broken neck."

So you proceed to start this crash course of self-defense. This goes on for several hours. Then she says you need to finish by a certain time because she has to be somewhere. This is fine for you because you are running out of sticks for her to break. So you stop. She is so grateful and excited for what she have learned.

You tell her before she goes in to shower and change clothes, "There is one last thing you need to learn."

She is in such a hurry that she figures she could learn it later.

You tell her mother, "She has to learn this now!"

Your aunt asks you, "What is it?"

You tell your aunt, "She has to learn about shock, freezing, and modesty."

You can see the reaction on your aunt's face. "Oh my God!" She covers her mouth with her hands. "That's why you wanted her to wear old clothes, so if they got torn in, it is no big deal because if she freezes them, she will lose her life!"

About that time, your cousin comes back outside all dolled up. She is late for the homecoming dance. You look at your aunt. She says, "Do it! Now you may not like doing this, but logically, it is necessary."

You walk up to your cousin who is showing off her very nice-looking new blouse. You tell her she looks fantastic. Then you reach up, grab, and then pull on her blouse. Yes, it tore! One mammary gland (breast) is exposed. Your cousin just stands there in shock. She is frozen. You have to push her for her to realize she is frozen or stunned.

After she thawed out and realized what you have done, she turns into the most vicious wildcat you ever saw. As she comes after you, she has blood in her eyes with vengeance. Quickly, you are trying to stay clear of her because an accident may occur, and you may get an unwanted broken bone. You are laughing so hard that you just made her madder. Wow, for a short time, she is actually faced with the real McCoy, "figure of speech." Her hair is now a mess. Her brand-new blouse is ripped, and one mammary gland is exposed. She is late for the dance.

Finally, you got her to calm down. Boy is she mad at you. She cleans up again, redresses, and says a few choice of words to you before she leaves in a hurry for the dance. Before you leave that evening, you talk to your aunt asking her to explain to her daughter that this has to happen.

"You tell her brother do not play around because if you surprise her, be very careful you could get hurt. No horse play."

Close to a month had gone by, you don't hear anything. You call your aunt to ask. She tells you that she will fill in all details at the family get-together next week. So that says something happened at the family gathering. Your aunt tells you that the three boys waited until after the race time. When she was on her horse behind the arena, they attacked by pulling her off her horse down to the ground. With a questionable suspense look on your face, you ask, "Well, what happened?"

"Your cousin very well defended herself. Her whole blouse and bra were ripped off. She was covered in dirt, hay, and horse manure. She did not care about modesty under the circumstances."

"Is she all right?"

"Yes, she is okay."

"What about the boys?"

"But the three boys are not."

"So what happened?"

"All three boys have several very serious physical injuries. They were all screaming in pain as they rolled around on the ground. First, an ambulance showed up. The boys were loaded up for major medical treatment. Then the law took them to jail after they were released from the hospital. Soon we will learn of a court date when we have to attend for a hearing."

About that time, your cousin arrives. With open arms, her face blushes red and eyes full of tears. You both stand there in a full embracing hug. You can feel her body shaking and hear her crying while you feel her tears running down your cheek.

"Thank you for teaching me how to defend myself."

"You're welcome."

Time passes. The court session is over. Your aunt once again calls and asks you to help one more time! "Your cousin is extremely emotionally upset from seeing the horrified faces. Eyes full of tears on the faces of the mothers of the three young men, knowing that each mother was there for their son."

As the judge passes sentence, she is watching each mother clasp to their seat after hearing the sentence their son has received and hearing the mothers cry out "Oh my God! No!" as their eyes flood with tears, watching their son as they are escorted out of the courtroom while hearing the chains between their feet rattle on the floor as they walk to the side door. As everyone is leaving the courtroom in tears, different people are saying they're so sorry.

"Please forgive us. Please forgive the three young men."

When you meet with your cousin, she is an emotional wreck. First thing, she shared a hug. You notice as you place your arms around her, there is no life in the hug. Then you sit down together side by side on the couch. You notice her face is so red, and her eyes are bloody shot. Her aroma is questionable. Her clothes are dirty while constantly wiping away her tears due to impulse crying.

"Would you like to talk about it?" She remains lifeless. "Okay, you don't have to talk. That's fine. You and I know that emotionally, we can wish it will go away, and everything will be fine. You and I know that does not happen, or logically, you can talk about the problem. 'A situation with an unknown solution.' Find and face the actual solution. Now here is the problem that has a situation where you are avoiding the solution. Logically, if you talk about the situation, face the situation. Then you can logically apply the solution because if you are looking for sympathy, you will find it in the dictionary between shit and suicide! Now you have a choice because right now, you are letting this problem tear you down. It will slowly destroy your life. Think about your future, marriage, kids, and your immediate family. Now I know you are very strong young lady. I know that you are happy with yourself. I know that you are a leader." You are talking and acting like a drill sergeant.

"Now you have a choice. You can let this destroy your future of life, of joy, and prosperity, or you can get up and rebuild what has been torn down. Remember life is short, and time is precious. The bottom line is, it was either you or them. No ifs and buts about it." All of a sudden, she slowly turns her head and gives you this look of "go to hell." You run out of words, so you just continue to sit there in total silence, enjoying each other's company.

Finally she starts to open up. You notice her mother who is present the whole time. Now you see her face glow with a huge smile and relief of worries. You become a good listener as she speaks of the thought she is dealing with.

"Why me?" she asks as tears fall. "Why did something like this happen to me?" Tears fall, and impulse crying starts.

You point out logically to her.

"You need to go to a rescue center for women. There, you can sit and listen to the other women. How they were just minding their own business at home, work, or a party. Listen to them as they tell their stories on how they were raped then beaten to a pulp then put in the hospital. They will ask the same question 'Why me?' Then listen to the women who were raped and left for dead. They will ask the same question 'Why me?' Logically, you can heal yourself by compassion to the other women. You and I know you are a leader. You have a choice. Someone helped you. Now you can help someone at the rescue center for women."

Time has passed. Guess where she went? Yes, you are right. To a rescue center for women. She finds the healing then helps other women heal. She is a role model for every woman. Now read this:

Do your Home Work: Get a second opinion: Do your research: Compare your options: Do you have a plan?

You can do the same in same form or passion

Women in Their Own Unique Way

They are the most beautiful creation God ever made.

While she was close to graduation, I would come home expecting to see a very good-looking, happy-go-lucky woman with a wonderful sense of humor, my sister. But when I would come home, I found a young woman who was moping around and often in tears with a sad, negative outlook. At first, I asked her, "What is wrong or what is bothering you?"

She would reply, "Nothing is wrong."

"How many times has this happened to you? Like you, I have seen this before."

So I said to my sister as I slowly took her into my arms and gently gave her a hug, "If you don't want to talk about it, that's okay with me. But I have a suspicion this is all about emotion because you are showing it. You may have forgotten about logic. So why don't you and I spend time together and go to the mall?" She looked at me with a flicker of light in her eyes.

"Okay, let's go," she said with a slight smile that followed. We reached the mall, gone inside, and just started walking around. Now I did not take her into any stores.

She kept looking at me and asked, "Why did you take me to the mall if we are not going into the stores to shop? Are you tired of walking around?"

"Yes, I am tired! Well, you probably are calculating we have walked around this mall three times. So why don't we just sit down over here on these benches?"

"Now are you going to tell me why we have walked around this mall three times?" she asked with a disgusted look on her face and tone of voice.

"Are you going to tell me what is bothering you?"

She looked at you with a very loud ___ of disgust.

"What is your point? Now I need you to think! Back at the house for the past three weeks, something emotional has been eating you alive! So logically, that's why I brought you to the mall to see if I can get you to open up. In the meantime, I will talk. If you don't want to talk, that's okay with me because you are only hurting yourself!

"While we sit here, don't be afraid to talk to your brother, or just pretend I am a friend. Now I am going to talk about women. I am asking you to be a good listener. If you have any questions or comments, by all means, speak up and ask. Okay, what are you trying to learn? I was raised up in a business environment. Now I am to say to be business-minded. I am single. Therefore, if I were to get married, logically, I would want to marry someone who is business-minded as well. For example, a wonderful woman who has parents who own and run a very successful business because logically, it would help our business take off faster and have a higher guarantee to be successful.

"But how will I find this person? Looking at their public appearance. How they hold themselves and how they stand—the look of self-confidence, liking themselves, and the look of success. Plus talking to them. Hear how much logic is in their dialogue. Besides, all we have today is the dating game that is on TV. So how else am I going to find this woman? Maybe I could put an ad in the newspaper. Now, sis, look at that woman standing over there to the right by that potted tree."

"Which one?"

"The one that is wearing that very tight jumpsuit. That looks very nice from here," I said in a low tone voice. Sis just rolled her eyes.

With a huge smile, I said, "I am going to talk to her with a sarcastic tone of voice, and just what are you going to talk about? A date? Maybe."

I walked over to her. I introduced myself and asked her if she would help me in a general survey. Of course, the young lady was a little surprised. She did enjoy the survey questions. Of course, I did accept her phone number. Now I went back to sit down by my sister. As she looked at me, she had a blushing facial expression with a huge smile.

"How was it?"

"That woman is very unique in her own way. She likes to feel comfortable in how people notice her by the clothes she wears. But her parents are an average blue-collar worker who live from paycheck to paycheck. Hey, sis! Look over there to the left and that woman standing by the half price sign. Now look at her style of dress."

Nice blue jeans and that blouse. It has ruffles. Somewhat plain and ordinary.

"Sis, okay. But look at those shoes she is wearing. Where do you think she bought them at, sis?"

"Well, those are top brand. They are not cheap! Those are expensive shoes. I bet she is someone in my category."

With an excited expression, I said, "Well, sis, I'll be right back."

I walked over to the young woman.

"Excuse me, but would you mind in helping me with a few questions? I am doing a survey as a science project. This will only take about two minutes. I hope to get a good grade."

She looked at you with a slight redness blushed face, a twinkle in her eyes, a slight smile, and a short laugh then said okay. So we talked for a few minutes, then she offered me her phone number. Yes, being polite, I accepted it. I had a huge smile on my face.

Sis asked me, "How many phone numbers do you have now?"

"Two at the moment."

"Yes, that woman is someone I would definitely want to get to know. Her parents own their own business. Yes, they are very successful. I am showing you about decisions. I want to have a happy harmonious marriage, a large family, and a good business partner. In a marriage, you make all kind of business decisions. Therefore, logically, I would pick the second woman I have talked to."

Now sis finally opened up to tell me what was bothering her. She said that when we are born and grow to young adults, some people have the physical appearance that everyone likes to look at.

"Yes, natural beauty, sis."

"Yes, then the problem is my girlfriends get mad at me because their boyfriends are more attracted to me than to them. So they get mad and start calling me names. I don't know how to handle it. It is not my fault."

"You are right. It is not your fault! Now in reality, due to natural beauty you are in appearance, a very beautiful woman, and people are going to look and stare at you because you are a fine piece of art that God created. So get used to it. Don't let it bother you because people admire fine art of beauty. Now I want to see a smile on your face. Right now!"

She leaned over and put her head on my shoulder. "Thank you."

"Look at me, where is the smile?"

She raised her head with tears in her eyes. She just smiled while wiping her tears.

"Now that's better. Do we have an understanding?"

"Yes, I understand. Thank you." Then she gave me this loving hug of happiness followed by an even bigger smile. As I hold her hand while one arm around her, I said, "Sis, there is something you are overlooking."

"What is that?"

"As my sister, you know I am always joking about emotional decisions versus logical decisions. I am always asking that question, right? Yes, and I get tired of it too! I did not know I was such of a bore to you."

"You're not. I was just kidding. You are a fantastic brother, and I love you very much. Thanks."

"What you are overlooking is, you speak with a lot of logical common sense. Yeah, that's because I am always around you. That's right. You have done a very good job of learning it. Sis, when you talk with logical common sense. That is very attractive to the male species. That magnifies the physical beauty of every woman who uses it. It attracts men like you would not believe. Now your girlfriends. Just remind your girlfriend's boyfriend that he is with her, not you. Of course, you may be flattered, but you are showing your friends respect. Reminding her boyfriend he is with her even if you tell him thank you for the compliment he gives you."

Sis started out with problem with an unknown solution. Working together, she realized she had a situation and a known solution which she did apply with fantastic results of gaining very high respect and gratitude from her friends and the boyfriends' girlfriends.

"Sis, I am really tired. Can we go now?"

With raised eyebrows on her face, I looked around at the people who were there with us in the mall. No, there was no more person I need to talk to. Sis looked at me with this long-face look.

"You must be kidding." I just looked at her.

She stopped and thought with a smile. "Okay."

"You see that young woman straight ahead of us?"

Sis replied, "You mean, the woman who is extremely overweight? Who is wearing an outfit as though she does not care and looking at her feet as she walks?"

"Yes, that one. We'll go talk to her." I walked directly to this woman. She saw me coming directly toward her. She stopped and just watched me walking up to her with a smile on my face.

She was looking at me like asking to herself, "What in the world is going on?"

"How are you doing?" She gave me this okay-so-far look. With a smile and polite body language, I asked her if she would not mind in helping me get a good grade on my science project by asking her a few questions of a survey.

She looked at me as I noticed her tongue was pushing against her cheek as it moved around from one side of her face to the other.

She replied with raised eyebrows, "Does your science project have anything to do with that very pretty brunette you were just sitting with?"

"Well, yes and no. Now you get this look if this is going to be a good one. First of all, that is my sister. The science project is to help her understand herself plus the knowledge she has. Plus the reaction of people to explain and understand why her friends are giving her a very hard time. Her girlfriends' boyfriends tend to be drawn toward my sister."

"I just can't imagine why. I must say she is a very beautiful-looking woman."

"Well, thank you. This problem does not go good with the girlfriends. In fact, it has gotten very ugly. I will bet it has."

Now the young lady saw and realized that as she was thinking. I was only talking to her to help my sister. You could see in her facial expression as it dropped with sad eyes the emotional disappointment and letdown she was feeling she showed in her voice and body posture. She did not appreciate the feeling of being used.

Now was she jumping to conclusions? Very quickly, I made a comment that I have read an article in a woman's magazine that when one person is feeling down, another person offers to share just a friendly hug to the person who is feeling down and that sharing a friendly hug is like a jumpstart for the rest of the day for the other person because it shows you care.

Looking at her face with a soft smile on her face, I said with a smile, "Would you be interested in sharing a warm just friendly hug?"

Her face lighted up. Her eyes were sparkling with a blushed smile.

"You know, you are very unique in your own way. With a smile, you are a very pretty woman."

"Yes, I believe I would be interested in this hug you have described."

You noticed she was feeling more at ease with herself as a light glow surrounded her body. As you were moving toward her, you embraced her in a smooth but firm, warm hug. As you held her in your arms, you continued to feel the emotion intensified as the softness of her body pressed against yours while the body temperature raised. That lasted for a good length of time. As you parted from the hug, her hand remained holding your hands. You noticed they are very moist and soft.

With a huge smile and sparkling eyes, she asked, "How is talking to me going to help your sister?"

"What kind of work do you do?"

"I am a cashier at a grocery store."

"What do you want out of life? For example, to move up in the corporate world, marry a fantastic man, have a happy family."

"I suppose you are going to tell me you have a magical wand that you can use to change a girl from rags into a girl like Cinderella?"

You just smile. "No, I don't have a magical wand, but what I do have is an additional 'avenue.'"

With a slight squeeze of her hands, a smile, and one raised eyebrow, she asked, "Oh, I have just got to hear this." With a humorous, skeptical tone of voice, she added, "I would not miss this for all the tea in China!"

"This is an avenue that has been right in front of us all along, but the reason we do not see it is because no one has pointed it out to us."

She was looking at you while still holding your hands with a very open mind and interested look.

"Please go on. I would like to hear more. What is it?"

"It is learning to think and speak when needed: LOGICAL COMMON SENSE."

You could see the curious interest in her facial expression.

"Would you mind explaining this to me?"

"I would be delighted to."

You explained to her about the two different languages we speak. How one is primary and how the secondary is formed. You also pointed out, as we age, how the secondary language is primarily used in the workforce and everyday life. You pointed out that in order to accomplish her goals with less resistance, she may want to consider trying and learning this method to see for herself the rewards it will bring. "Is this something you teach?"

"Yes, I do." Her face lighted up with delight. "When could we get started? By all means, I would really look forward to you personally teaching me this new 'avenue' as you call it."

"You have a family member that can also teach you."

You can't help but notice a look of disappointment in her face and eyes.

"Well, can we stay in touch in case I have any questions?"

"Yes, of course."

Her face lighted back up as she quickly removed her hands from yours and very quickly wrote her phone number then placed it in your shirt pocket. Then she quickly grabbed your hands again.

"If you ask your family member and work together, he will teach you, and both of you will learn so much. Then actually you will end up with more laughter than before. Now it is up to you!"

"So you're saying I need to learn the difference between making emotional decisions versus logical decisions?"

"Logical common sense."

"What is one of the biggest rewards of learning and using this?"

"This is one of the most attractive things to the male species. From there, it splits off to respect, appreciation, and intensifies beauty and leadership."

"Well, I hope that you can help your sister by talking to me."

"Oh, yes! I will help my sister, but I hope in return I was able to help you."

"I believe you have. Can I have your phone number? Thank you."

"You're welcome."

"Okay, you have mine right here in your shirt pocket next to your heart," she said showing a very flirty smile. "That was a very nice hug we shared as when we first met," she added with a very lovable look. "Is there a parting hug included?" She raised her eyebrows with a smile.

"Why, of course."

You noticed that the two of you came into contact a little quicker. Slowly, both of you raised out your arms then stepped forward to come into contact with each other. As she slid her arms around your upper body, you noticed she was firmly squeezing her hold. You have slid your arms around her. She was rubbing her hands up and down your back. You can feel her very soft yet very warm body pressing against yours. You raised your right hand up between her hair and neck as you do the same by massaging her neck. Your left hand had moved to her lower back. You noticed the aroma of white diamonds to intensify. As this smooth, firm, emotional hug lasted, it ended with a very moist parting kiss. Looking at her blushed face, soft eyes, and sweet smile, you smiled goodbye. Her eyes were filling with tears then softly said goodbye.

You walked back over to your sister. She looked at you with a smile and two raised eyebrows. "Wow! Look at you. Well, let's see. You have three phone numbers from three different women. You have shared two hugs from one woman following up with a long kiss, what's next?"

You just smiled with raised eyebrows and shrugged shoulders.

"I don't know what to say. Are you ready to go home?"

"Let's do it!"

Do your Home Work: Get a second opinion: Do your research: Compare your options: Do you have a plan?

Unexpected Things Happen

About two years later, your wife and you are shopping at the same mall in the town. As you go from store to store to shop, at the last store of candles, you tell your wife you are going to stand outside the store there in the isle of the mall.

Your wife says, "Okay, because it will take a minute for what I need to take care of."

"Okay, I will be right here."

Now you are minding your own business watching people walk by as they are headed to different stores, and you turned to see your wife up at the cashier line close to the front of the store. You're thinking, *Great, now we can leave because this was the last stop.* All of a sudden, to your surprise, there are two very moist, soft hands covering each of your eyes as you feel a very warm body press very firmly against your back all the way down your back. You can't help but notice a strong different aroma of perfume "white diamonds." You know this is not your wife's VERA WANG. You find yourself PARALYZED. You are trying to stay calm because if you could see your wife in the store, that means she can see you. *I hope she is not looking!* Your heart is pounding out of your chest, and your body temperature is going through the roof. As you notice the sweat running down each side of your face, the two little soft, moist hands were removed from your eyes.

The first thing that comes into focus is your wife just looking at you with both hands on each hip. You are past being stunned. You are trying to smile at your wife knowing chaos is about to happen. You are thinking of what you're going to say to your wife.

"Baby, this is not what you think. Just trust me," you say with a sweet smile and tilt of the head because the look on her face is "Oh, you are going to pay big-time. You're dead!"

"What is going on here?" All of a sudden, this very radiant of glowing area and this beautiful woman whose hair is beautifully styled with wonderful application of makeup, sparkling eyes, and a beautiful smile looking like a doll, stepped out then slide in front of you.

"Do you remember me?" You smile at the lovely, attractive woman while still noticing your wife standing ten feet away. You turn to your wife and give a hand signal. "Just a minute."

As you notice the look on her face, it says, "Just go right ahead because I'm going to give you all the rope you need to hang yourself with. I would like to see how you're going to get out of this one." You turn your attention back to the young woman. You do not even recognize her. You can see a little bit of laughter in her facial expression because she just watches you on how you handle the situation with your wife.

"Pretty good show." So with a charming smile, you are trying to slow down your heart rate and bring down your body temperature while wiping the sweat off your face.

With a smile, you mention to the woman, "I have talked to a lot of people, so if you don't mind, could you give me a hint as to where and when the two of us met and what we spoke of?"

"Two years ago, we met right here at this very spot. You were telling me the value and rewards of learning to think and speak with logical common sense. You were helping your sister with an issue of her own."

You stand there thinking about a woman you met two years ago. You may mostly rely on remembering her appearance first. Think. *Did I really meet this person before because I sure couldn't remember!* I do remember a woman who did not care much for a nice wardrobe probably because she was carrying more body weight than she wanted. Her hairstyle was just a washed dry and comb and was only interested in all-natural face appearance who was a cashier at a grocery store. There were not many men asking to court her. Now two years later, she has done a total makeover. She is the district manager over all the hand jewelry stores of the two local malls plus has many men asking to court her.

She asks, "Are you in the mall alone?"

"No," you answer with "I-am-in-trouble" smile.

"I wish I could have met you sooner! Is that your wife standing there?"

You nodded your head with a half of a smile. "Yes."

"I always wanted to show and tell you of my appreciation for what you did for me."

"Well, I am very glad you have accomplished your goals."

"Thank you. I am engaged to get married."

"Well, congratulations."

"Would it be all right to give you a very special, nice, warm hug as to show my appreciation?"

You're thinking, *OH YEAH! And my wife is standing right there.* So you figured you are already in hot water, but this woman is asking this of you as a sincere request.

"Yes, that would be nice." So you and the woman slide your arms around each other. She has slowly and gently slide her arms under yours. Then to your surprise, she gives you a very firm, tight hug. You can't help but to feel all of her body pressing against yours. The whole time, you are thinking, *My wife is going to kill me.*

All of a sudden, the radiant woman grabs your ears with each hand and pulls your face forward. Then she lays a very moist and warm kiss on your lips as your arms shoot to the ceiling due to the total unexpected event. Now logically, you know you are in hot water with your wife. You don't want to disappoint the radiant woman. So what do you do?

Well, you cannot help but to notice the radiant woman's extremely moist wet lips are all over your mustache and face. So you match her style of kissing. Again, you want to please this woman with the passion she desires. So you do the same thing you do to your wife when you and her are sharing a moment of intimate love and affection. You slowly bring your hand up into her hair right at the base of her neck, giving her a smooth gentle massage. Then very smoothly, you bring both hands down her shoulders and very gently massage her all the way to her sides. But not to far forward below her shoulders. Then you lower your hands and gently massage just above the hips. When all of a sudden, she intensifies body pressure of the body hug.

Now finally, you and the radiant woman part. Your heart never did slow down. Your body temperature just go up several more degrees. You still have sweat to wipe off your face. You feel like you had just gone through a workout. With this look, she says in a very sexy panting voice "Thank you" as she is fanning herself.

"Why, you are quite welcome. If you don't mind, I would like to ask you for a small favor."

She leans toward you and smiles. "Anything?"

You smile and take a deep breath as she leans closer to you. "Yes."

"Would you mind if you would explain this all to my wife because she will believe you before she will believe me."

"Why, of course. I will talk to her."

She turns and talks to your wife privately while you stand ten feet away. Then she turns, looks at you giving a sexy one-eye wink followed by a sexy blow kiss of goodbye as she walks off with style.

Now what did the wife do?

If she would have handled this issue with emotion, most likely, she would have cursed me out up one side and down the other very loudly there in public. She may have physically consulted the other woman. Plus tell me I am sleeping on the couch, no, better yet, in the freaking garage.

"No, you know what? Just pack your luggage, and get out of the house. Find your own way home. You are walking."

Then she stomp while wiping her eyes as tears fall in front of me. "How could you!" As she heads toward the car in the parking lot.

Due to logical common sense, I gave my wife a lot of credit, respect, and admiration because she has learned over the years I have helped a lot of people in the past. She just met and listened to a person give her live testimony that would bring tears to your eyes. A total life makeover story where they went from extremely overweight, low-career job, and a boyfriend that would not stay. This brought her self-esteem down right into the gutter with a little light insight. All through this time, she did not give up. Like many people, she prays to God asking him for help. An answer, guidance, and someone to show her the way to better change her life in the world. Then one day, when she least expected it, we meet in the mall while I was in the process of helping my sister. Of all places, the day I was going to help my sister. Why did I pick that mall?

After the conversation is over between your wife and the radiant woman, you see your wife standing there alone looking at you. Now you are wondering how hot the water that you are in is. So you see her smiling at you with her eyes full of tears. She gracefully walks over to you and put her arms around your waist. "Mister, let's go home and live happily after!"

What did that woman say to your wife? You still don't know!

Do your Home Work: Get a second opinion: Do your research: Compare your options: Do you have a plan?

Never Make a Permanent Decision on a Temporary Emotion

The Coworker

Each job, the employer has his own safety rules he has how to follow. When you are on the job and the company hires new people, these people bring different ideas and methods from their previous job.

"Here is the case" for the man classified as a pipe fitter. He was used to using a choker to use to lift a piece of pipe and move to the overhead crane. His method was to use what is called a basket. This looks a *U*-shape. When using this method, there should be two cranes. Now the fitter was holding the crane controls in one hand while balancing the pipe with his other hand. This was a large piece of pipe. Reality, it is and can be very dangerous because the pipe can slide or slip right out of the strap (choker) because it is not locked around the pipe. Now this was what he used to do at his previous employer. That seemed to have been allowed.

Every day, we have a safety meeting. The fitter and the whole group of employees were informed by the safety coordinator that this was forbidden at this company. He was informed of the new employer's policy. One day, not thinking the fitter had to move at a big diameter roughly four feet long piece of pipe that he was working on, the fitter got the overhead crane over the pipe he needed to move. He then placed the choker under the pipe in the "figure of speech" the old way. A supervisor was watching this. The fitter reached for the hand controls of the crane with intention to lift and move the pipe with the crane. The supervisor yelled "No!" as he hurried over to the fitter to stop him from lifting the pipe because of the unsafe rigging.

"Question:" how is the fitter going to react? He reacted startled, and you could see the emotional expression on his face. The supervisor was trying not to use a deep concern with a harsh tone of voice. Immediately, the supervisor was reminding the fitter, "This is very unsafe. You could injure someone, damage something, or injure yourself."

The fitter immediately and with high emotion responded with the high tone of voice, "This is how I have done this for years at my last job!"

The supervisor was getting emotional because there was an argument starting to take place.

So the supervisor told the fitter, "All right, come with me!"

"Where are we going?"

"To the safety department. We will inform them of this event and let them decide."

"Let them decide what?"

"If they are going to (1) write you up, (2) give you time off, or (3) fire you."

The fitter was getting very emotionally upset considering he just got hired two weeks ago. Now he was in his eyes fixing to lose his job.

When the other supervisors were contacted, they sat down to discuss the ordeal with the fitter. The fitter was still handling this situation with high emotion. Talking very loudly, he told the supervisor what they can do with their policy following with a hand signal of profanity! At this point, the supervisors were trying to handle this logically. Still dealing with the emotion due to what the fitter said and his hand signal, they chose to terminate the fitter with no chance of rehire.

Now let's look at the situation. If it would have been handled as a logical decision, the fitter would've possibly handled it this way. Yes, he used the old way of habit. But when the supervisor startled him, he should've just let the supervisor speak "and keep his mouth shut" and let the supervisor speak and calm down.

"Yes, sir. You are absolutely right! I do apologize for my actions of negligence from my previous employer. Yes, sir, remembering this is not allowed here at this company. It will not happen again, sir. I will immediately change the rigging to the company expectations, sir."

There's a very good chance everything would have stopped here. The supervisor would have appreciated the respect and the act of knowledge of the fitter. Most likely, the fitter would not have been written up, given time off, or fired. The fitter would have kept his job. If this was you, the fitter, how would you handle this situation?

Do your Home Work: Get a second opinion: Do your research: Compare your options: Do you have a plan?

Never Make a Permanent Decision on a Temporary Emotion
Weigh out the consequences of Emotion, to the rewards of logic

That High School Sweetheart

Remember your senior year of high school when you were spending most of your time with one young lady? Remember how the two of you would constantly talk on the phone because she had to go home, and you have to go home after school? Remember when she would invite you over for supper, so her father and mother could meet you? Oh yeah! You remember the looks you used to get from her parents! Remember how it seemed how one of the parents did not approve of you as if you were not good enough for their daughter because of your dress code, lifestyle, or grade point average (GPA). Ideas in life as you spent time being around her parents, you generally found different things that you did not like or agree with on how the parents were treating your sweetheart as they raised her, or you may not agree on how they look at you as to your potential of being a good suitor for their daughter. There are millions of young men who all went through this.

Now remember when this happened to you! As a young adult, by watching our parents logically, we had it all figured out about life and living a life as a couple. But we overlooked the part about our career and her career because it took most couples to both have a good paying job in order to pay the bills that are going to come. This is one of the main things parents are so concerned with and drill into the heads of children. No, you may not approve of the method the parents were using.

As you look back on your sweetheart and other girlfriends, there was generally a lot of static between the mother and the daughter, especially during the mid-to-late teen years. This was something that all guys got to hear about from their sweetheart. Oh, my parents this. Oh, my parents that. You were so tired of this and them as they were crying on the phone while talking to you. So I ask you, "Why does this happen?"

Whatever the reason, it does and is going to continue to happen. The only thing you can do is just deal with it. Funny thing dealing with it. Think about the times when your emotions of all of this was reaching a boiling point. That's right. Your boiling point! You would just get so mad. Now you just want to voice your opinion to her parents. But logically, you realize you need to be respectful to her parents. So you bite your tongue while your blood pressure is going off the chart because of the feeling you have for her. When one person close to you gets upset, then you start getting upset. You hope that the parents will change, but they will not. Hope this will go away, but it will not. You hope the arguments between your sweetheart and her parents will stop because it is driving you crazy. You try to deal with your life and whatever problems you have. But now, this extra extreme weight of your sweetheart is pulling you down. This affects you at school and working around customers. Example, when you're working at fast-food restaurant, not to mention when you are around your parents.

Remember as you look back on this! Just how rude and disrespectful you were to your parents. Do you remember how your parents were trying to help you deal with this situation? But you also remember that at this age, you knew everything there was to know about life. Did you listen to your parents or just listen to them? You let them know you had it all under control, but did you really think? Well, you probably did, and you came to the conclusion that there was only one way to solve this problem because you have tried everything you could think of. Even though you have learned and mostly used logic to make your decisions, you forgot the first language and method of decisions is emotion because no one took the time to teach you that we operate and make decisions based on the two different languages and thought. Therefore, we don't know the best time to use the correct thinking when we are faced with a crisis just how important making a decision is.

There was this night. Yes, my son was experiencing the same thing dealing with possible future in-laws. He would come home depressed. He would be grouchy and grumpy. He even got to where he was being disrespectful that when I would have to remind him of his lack of manners. Both his mom and I would ask him to talk to us, not as parents but as friends. Maybe we can help. Yes, he did talk to us, and yes, we did help. But you and he knew that this was not going to solve the problem.

One reason was because the wonderful sweetheart was calling your son, telling him that right now, she was in a crisis with her parents. She was crying because she was just not sure of what to do. "Bless her heart." You remember puppy love? She was emotionally upset that she's talking about her feelings toward your son and goals in life. But she was being led and educated or controlled by her parents. She felt that she cannot do anything under the circumstances due to her parents. At this point, do you remember what you did? My son was thinking that yes, he was going to resolve this problem. His blood pressure was extremely high. He was all railed up because he has deep feelings for his girl.

I had met her father previously. I saw him as a leader, an entrepreneur, and was aware of his desire toward success. One night, my son and I were home. My son was in a very crabby mood. I was already aware of his situation concerning his girlfriend. I thought she is a fantastic, bright, and sharp person. So that night, as I was watching TV, I noticed my son was constantly coming out of his room then going back several times like he was pacing the floors as he would spend time in the kitchen fixing himself something to eat. I could not help from hearing the cabinet doors being slammed, the ice box door being slammed, and the silverware drawer slammed. As the plate was put on the counter, I was wondering if it got broken. I hollered, "Hey, take it easy on the merchandise. Settle down." Then a few minutes later, he came into the living room where I was at and slammed his boots on the floor and thrust one foot into a boot.

Then he thrust his other foot in the other boot and slammed his cap on to his head as if he were expecting a gust of high wind to blow it off his head. He jumped up and started stomping down the hall toward the front door. I hollered, "Wo-wo-wo. Where are you going?" He stopped and turned around.

In a very loud voice, he said, "Dad, I have had it!" He threw his arms and hands on the air. "I am trying everything. I am trying to help her." I watched the tears fill his eyes. "Dealing with rude customers at my fast-food job and her dealing with the issue she is having with her parents. Calling me telling me about it while crying her eyes out! Dad." He threw his hand on the air while showing deep emotion for her with his face red and moisture flooding his eyes. "Dad, I cannot take it anymore."

"So okay, you are right. But just what are you fixing to do right now?"

"Dad, I am going to go to her house and get her out of that situation. Tell her parents just what I think this is how it is. I will fix the whole thing."

"What else?"

"Her dad, and I may just have to physically fight." He wiped his tears that have been rolling down his face and tried to stop the tears that are following.

"Son, hey. I appreciate you stopping in the hall before you got to the door and came back in here and sat down. I am very proud of you for that. Now let just take a few moments, and let us just talk (1) as your dad and (2) as a friend."

"Okay, okay."

"Now you know, I have asked you this question all the time. At which you should be asking yourself all the time. You are fixing to make a very, very important decision. Now is it basing on emotion? Or is it basing on logic?" You can see he is calming down.

"Well, Dad."

"Son, let's take a few minutes and review this. Then whatever you decide to do, you have to live with. Right now, you are and have been getting very emotional. So if you carry out what you are thinking to do, you need to view the consequences versus the rewards. Right now, you have no place in the situation between your sweetheart and her parents!

"Understand there are consequences of making an emotional decision: (1) if you go over there and do the things you have mentioned, then you will cause damage that NEVER will be fixed or forgotten! (2) You will hurt people's feelings as well as your own. (3) This may turn out to where people are physically injured as well as yourself. (4) Most likely, you will end up in jail! So don't expect me to come and bail you out, or even worst thing can happen. It could be fatal!

"Now let's look at the logical decision: (1) Her parents are raising her the best way they know how! (2) They are her guardians. (3) That is their home. (4) What she is having to deal with is not all bad because one day, she will be out in the real world.

"So if she can deal and handle this like all young women in their teens, then they are going to handle the real world with ease. Also, she has been handling this issue for all the past years, anyway. You don't know every detail of what is actually going on. Details are so important in everything. So let it be. One day, you are a parent. You are going to look back at this night by the decision you make right now! You will either spare your son from doing something stupid or fatal or regret for the rest of your life saying, 'I could've done better!'"

Looking straight at him while watching tears run down his face, I added, "So now what are you going to do?"

He looked at me as he wiped the tears off his red face. He got up out of the chair he was sitting on, walked over me, gave me a big bear hug, and said, "Thanks, Dad."

As I was trying to hide the tears that are forming in my eyes, I replied, "You're welcome. I will talk to her tomorrow at school." He sat back down and took off his boots and cap. He then asked me if I need anything to drink.

"Yes, I would like a Coke." As he went for the drink, I was clearing my sinuses and drying my eyes.

"Dad," he asked from a distance, "are you all right?"

"Yes, I think I am coming down with a cold, or it is the dust in the air." He walked back, handed me my drink with his swollen red facial expression, and wiped his tears.

"Thanks, Dad."

"You're welcome." Then he returned to his room to work on his computer.

Do your Home Work: Get a second opinion: Do your research: Compare your options: Do you have a plan?

Never Make a Permanent Decision on a Temporary Emotion
Love lifted me

Selling Chocolate Bars

Remember when you were in school, and they had some kind of a sale to help raise money for the school? Remember how you participated? During this time, you may or may not have had your parents' moral support. Remember for the most part, you had to have your parents' permission because your parents had to buy the stuff before you sold it or if you took the order to sell this amount, and you did not sell all. Then your parents would have to pay the school the difference that you did not sell.

Now also remember when you were pretty young. How you used to ask your parents to sell this for you at their job? That was easy for you. It worked for a while! But did you even think your parents got tired of this? That's right. Tired of it! Drum roll. Remember when your parents told you, "Now you're old enough to sell your own stuff! I am not going to sell your stuff anymore!" Remember the thought that went out your mind?

Now I raised my children. They said I raised them as if I were a military drill sergeant! Now I don't see it that way. Yes, I raised them by being a little stern. Maybe a little direct. I thought I was a laid-back, easy-going coach.

My son came home all excited from school one day. "Dad, at the school, they are having a chocolate bar sale. They want all of us kids to sell this candy for band." Yes, he was in band. "Will you take these bars to your work and sell them for me? Hu-hu please," he said with a sweet little innocent smile. "Please, Dad? It's for my band at school!"

Now his mother asked him, "How much money does it cost per box if you do not sell any bars?"

My son replied, "Well, Mom, each bar only cost one dollar. Like it is no big deal."

"Okay, how many bars are in a box?"

Slowly and softly, he said, "Only fifty."

His mother blurted out, "Only fifty. That means each box cost fifty dollars if you do not sell them! How many boxes did you sign up for?"

Very slowly, he replied, "Only two."

His mother said "Oh my God!" in a loud, direct voice. "That means if you do not sell them, I am going to be out one hundred dollars. I am going to be eating a lot of chocolate bars. Now let me remind you, money is tight—very tight." The look he had on his face in the beginning was priceless with an excitement and self-confidence.

Now his mother meant well. But now due to emotion, the look on his face and his self-confidence was shattered. Thinking logically, I told my son while smiling and with a humorous laugh, "Son, you are about to take a class and learn. Dealing with the public. 'Public relations.'"

His face lit up and glowed as his eyes sparkled.

Then he asked, "Dad, what is public relations?"

So I told him, "Grab your boxes, and let's go."

With excitement, he replied, "Okay, Dad. Where are we going?"

"We are going to Walmart."

"Dad, it is 6:00 p.m."

"Yes, and it is Friday. You are going to need to show your manners. You need to change your clothes."

"What is wrong with what I am wearing?"

"Because you look like a slob. You know and I know everyone has to learn the hard way, but this is the best teacher."

When we got to the store, I told him we are going to meet the manager and ask permission to do this. So we did. I informed the manager that if any customers come in and complain, we will stop immediately and apologize to him personally, but we will do our best to have customers come in to compliment him for allowing this to happen.

Now as we are about to start, I asked my son, "What are you going to say to each person that walks up to the door where you are standing while holding your box of candy?"

"Dad, I don't think I can do this."

"*Can't* is not in our vocabulary. Try again."

With a very scared look on his face and with a little shaking, he said, "I don't know. All right, I will be standing right here about eight feet away from you.

"So no worries. I am here to protect you at all times. Now when these people you do not know come up to where you are standing, I will give you a hint. Talk to them the same way you would talk to your teacher at school. Emotionally, you are scared of strangers. Logically, feel comfortable because you know them. (1) You are to greet with a big smile. (2) Everything is 'Yes, ma'am,' 'No, ma'am,' 'Yes, sir,' and 'No, sir.' Is that clearly understood?"

"Yes, sir!"

"Now the only way you are going to learn is put one foot in front of the other foot and try."

The customers walked up. You could clearly see he was nervous. They liked his manners but disliked his dress, cap, and hair. There was one woman in particular that clearly showed this with expression. With a smile on my face, I quickly walked over to this woman.

"Ma'am, yes, you are absolutely right about not dressing for the occasion."

The look on her face went from disapproval seeing her eyebrows very close to her eyes to a stunned look of acknowledgment and respect that she is right.

"Well, thank you, sir."

"You must be his dad. Yes, ma'am."

"Ma'am," with this excited smile, I said, "would you be interested in helping this young man learn something very educational at which he will always be thankful in memory to you?"

Her face quickly lightened to a glow, her eyes started to sparkle, and a smile formed. She was looking at you like "Woah! I don't know what I did. But I must have done something good."

"Sir, I don't understand what you are asking." My son's face, you can see a troubled emotional look on his face. He was scared he is in trouble, not only from me but the store manager."

"Yes, he does look awfully scared and upset. Yes, ma'am."

"What can I do?"

"Ma'am, I am asking you to go over to him and explain to him why it is very important to dress for the right occasion the same way you would coach your son."

Now, girls, I give them credit. They are a little sharper and faster. You could see her face shine. Now boys are not always the sharpest tack in the shack. But once something is pointed out to them in a nice, constructive way of polishing, then they will become the sharpest tack in the shack.

"What do you say?" She had the look of amusement all around her beautiful smile.

"Yes, sir, I would be honored to help coach your son."

"Thank you, ma'am."

So the woman went over and talked to my son about how important it is to be clean, use a nice cologne, and be well-dressed for a presentation. When the woman first approached my son, you can see a scared look on his face while his eyes were filling with tears. After the woman talked to him, you could see him wipe his tears, change his standing posture, and then show increase of self-confidence, parting with a smile on his face respect and admiration to the woman followed by a handshake.

"Thank you, ma'am."

"You're very welcome," she replied as she entered the store. He did sell a few bars in three hours. ·

I finally told him, "Let's wrap it up and go home." He was getting discouraged at the slow sales but wanted to continue trying that night.

*****

Saturday night, he said, "Are we going to go back and try again, Dad?"

"Yes, there are some things you are going to have to do first."

"What's that dad?"

"(1) Get in there and take a shower! (2) Put on your good school clothes! (3) Use some gel in your hair and comb. (4) Put on some cologne. Now you do that, and we will try again!"

"Yes, sir," he replied, showing to be eager with excitement. He came out of his room all groomed up.

"Are you ready for round 2?"

"Yes, sir. I am ready. Let's go, Dad."

We arrived at the parking lot. My son was so eager to get started. He already had the car door half open before I had fully stopped to park. "Hold it. Not so fast."

"What's the matter, Dad? Do you have a logical game plan? Do I need a different one than the one I have?"

"Let's review last night. The reactions of the people you talked to. Let's see if you can see the need to polish your presentations. How are you going to greet the people? Let's start with the men. What are you going to say, and how are you going to say it? Example, talk to them like they are your coach or friend. You go by their age. The women, are you going to talk to them like they are your teacher at school? Your mother, your sister, or the girls at your school?"

"All of the above, Dad."

Then we rehearsed his presentation. He sold the remaining chocolate bars plus tips for his manners being well-dressed and presentation in three and a half hours. Now was he happy seeing and experiencing his success? You guessed it right. Yes!

Resurrection

The following year, he came home from school. "Dad, Dad, because of your guidance in helping me sell two boxes of chocolate bars last year, I know I can sell ten boxes this year."

"Do you have a plan?"

"Yes, sir."

"Let's hear it!" With a very confident teaching look on his face and tone of voice, he said, "Dad, logically, I do need to dress neatly and wear a smile with cologne. My hair looking neat, I need to show my manners. I need to address each person with total respect and show dignity. I have learned to think and speak two different languages between speaking to men and women. From trial and error, I have found the best logical thing to say. Now I know I can do this because of last year's success. Now selling five hundred bars of chocolate, there is no problem."

"Well, I am very proud of you." His smile widened. The glow on his face intensified, and his eyes sparkled.

"Thanks, Dad." He reached over to give me a hug.

"Now there is something you need to keep in mind about the people you talk to at the Walmart each night. They have been at work all day. They are tired and probably don't really want to be out shopping. They would rather be home resting from their long day. So keep in mind they are and can be a little crabby."

"Oh, you mean like Mom after she comes home from working a twelve-hour shift then has to go to Walmart?"

"That's right." There was a look on his face. "Oh, well, Dad, you are like that sometimes too!" He had a slight soft voice as he slowly looked upward to me. Then all of a sudden, he smiled with eyes high.

"You are right again. One more thing, the candy in the store is cheaper than your chocolate bars. So keeping all of this in mind, what are you going to say to the customers to convince them to want to buy your chocolate bars?"

"Well, Dad, I will definitely give this some thought!"

"Okay."

Here, I wanted to point out that my wife is a fantastic person. She is a wonderful mother to our son, so I do not have any intention to degrade her. Now money was tight again! She was coming home tired after a long drive from her job of working twelve-hour shifts. My son was excited and wanted to tell her all about his idea that has been carefully planned, learning to polish his method from trial and error which gained him great success.

People don't always say what they mean or say one thing when actually, they are saying something else. Say what you mean to say, not what you think to say. It could be your mom, dad, a relative, or a friend. There are times when someone, by the way they say something to you, you will either glow like a breaker or you feel like a crystal glass that just hit the floor and shuttered into a hundred pieces and also feel like you just got punched in the stomach! Remember? Now it is possible my son took it the wrong way. After telling his mother about his great plans, how he was going to sell the maximum allowed by the school which is ten boxes, five hundred bars, costing one dollar per piece, his mother made many comments!

He may have just taken what and how she made her comments the wrong way. Either way, the look on his face started out with a glow of excitement of confidence. Then slowly, the look melted on his face to a crystal glass that just hit the floor, shuttering into a hundred pieces. His eyes filled with tears.

Remember when something like this happened to you? Remember how emotionally upset you become? Yes, you were very upset, surprised, and letdown feeling like a failure because your confidence in yourself just got shut down. The answer is yes. It had happened to all of us! I was watching this take place as my son's eyes were filling with tears. He tried to slowly went to his room before his tears started rolling down his face.

I said to my wife, "I know you are tired from your twelve-hour shift. He had waited all day to tell you this exciting news, but you really need to think about how you say things because people can definitely take what you said the wrong way. Even though you meant it a different way."

"I am sorry. He will be okay. I will explain to him what I meant to clear up the misunderstanding."

"Yes, you definitely need to do that! I will go and check on him."

He was in junior high school. I walked into his room seeing his face red. Using a face rage wiping away his tears, he looked up at me.

"Dad, why!" He wiped his tears. Now I really got my job cut out for me as a parent. I was going to need to explain to my son how he was on top of the world of self-confidence of logic, but now he was in the gutter of emotion. The next day, I picked him up from school. He was standing in front of the band hall with two boxes of candy. I pulled up and saw a discouraged look on his face.

"Where are the other boxes?"

"Mister said I can only have two of the ten. After I sell two, then I can get two more."

"Let me park the car. Let's go talk to Mr. Who is over this." I found Mister. I talked to him. After the conversation was over, my son and I put all ten boxes into the car. As we were driving home, I noticed my son was quiet with a sour look on his face.

"What's wrong?"

"Nothing."

"Are you ready with excitement to do this big goal?"

"I do not care anymore. I am just a failure." Remember how depressed you become because your ego was shot down sometime in your life? So drive home. He didn't say much. I didn't talk anymore. I was thinking, *What is the most logical thing to do to get him back on track?* While a few hours have passed, the outside temperature was cooling down. I walked into my son's room where he was playing video games. I looked at his face to see old tears. Yes, he was still emotionally upset. He was letting the emotion consume him.

"Son, clean up, comb your hair, put on some cologne, and let's go get something to eat."

So he cleaned up his face, took a shower, changed clothes with cologne, and combed his hair. We went to Jack in the Box. Here I was explaining to him about people and how they react under different circumstances. Different things affect different people in different ways. Sometimes good, sometimes bad.

"You have to learn how to shield yourself from the bad effects because if you don't, it will ruin your plans to be successful toward your goals." He started to lighten up. Yes, his self-confidence was rising.

Then all of a sudden, he said, "Dad, thanks, but between Mom and some of my friends, I just don't care anymore. Can we go home now?"

I looked at him thinking, *Is he going to continue to walk in the ditch of self-destruction?* Logically, I needed to somehow pull him out. *How?*

"Dad, can we just go home now?"

"While we are here, do you want to sell some chocolate bars?"

"No, I don't think I can sell anything at all. Can we go now? I just want to go home."

His face was long with a look of pity. And do what "loudly" watching, okay.

"Let's go." So we got up. I put my arm around on his shoulder as we walked to the car. After in the car, I turned and looked at him. You could see on his eyes and facial expression asking himself, *What am I doing? Mr. Dad supports me while other pull me down. What do I do? Quit or go forward?*

Then as we were driving, he had a shocked look on his face. "You are going the wrong way."

"Yes, because the house is that way." As he pointed, I just turned, and looked at him with a smile on my face.

"Yes, you're right. Dad, where are we going?" You should've seen the look on his face as I pulled into the Walmart parking lot.

The look on his face was "Oh no!" His eyes got large as his mouth opened, and his chin fell on his lap. With a large lump on his throat, he tried to swallow.

After parking, I said, "Now I am going to talk. You are going to listen. You started with a goal to sell two boxes of candy bars last year. You put one foot in front of the other. You learned from trial and error. You become successful! Now this year, you are going to do the exact same thing because of your well-established plan you used last year." Loudly, with a very stern voice, I added, "I am going to say this one time: you have a choice to make. You can make the choice of logic. Sell all ten boxes and accomplish your goal that has already been proven to work, or you can make the decision of emotion and quit or give up! But let me inform you of the consequences of emotion. You and I are going to go through a course of boot camp. Do I make myself clear?"

With fear in his eyes, he replied, "Yes, sir."

"Now you have to count of three to decide!"

The look on his face was "oh my God. I need to get cracking!" One pause, two. I noticed he was already out of the car way before I got to say three. As we were getting out of the car, there were several other people getting out of their vehicles. Now I know I have made a scene. Just seeing all of these people just staring at us with the look of cautious curiosity on their faces. My son was trying to hide his tears. So I proudly looked at all the people who walked over to my son while he held two boxes.

"Stop!" My son froze. "I figured since I am making a scene, I might as well make a good one." Speaking loud and very firmly, I walked over to my frozen son, placed my arm around his shoulders taking one box from him, and told him to place his arm on my shoulder. Then real loudly, I said, "Okay. Now in step, side by side. We are going in step to march to the door of the store. Now follow along as I say. We will start our march on the count of three. Hop one, hop two, hop three."

We start our march in step side by side both saying:

"I've been told two working together can have a goal!
I've been told two working together can have success.

136

I've been told two working together can reach a goal."
As we marched to the doors, last step. "I've been told, Ooh rah!"

I looked at my son's face to see admiration and excitement with a glow of self-confidence with a sparkle in his eyes and a smile a mile wide. Then we noticed that we had an audience who applauded us as to see a rare performance of a father and son spending time together. This was a special Kodak moment. My son addressed the store manager to thank him for all he did. Then he proceeded to sell his chocolate bars. He sold all ten boxes "five hundred bars" and received many large tips for his performance. This was done in three-and-a-half nights lasting three to four hours.

Do your Home Work: Get a second opinion: Do your research: Compare your options: Do you have a plan?

The Den Leader Mentality
High Mentality versus Low Mentality

High mentality is where one can think and solve problems very quickly because their thinking ability is at very large range of remembering, learning, reasoning, etc. Example "McIvor."

Low mentality is where a person tries but due to the lack of knowledge can have a very low range of thinking.

There is a saying "think outside the box." The question is how big is the box you are trying to think outside? Either way, the definition of low mentality according to the dictionary is an idiot. Now a young boy goes from feeling due to the lack of knowledge "I am an idiot" to the high mentality of a late teenager. The boy is ten years old.

This all began one year when you take up the job as a den leader over a group of nine-to-eleven-year-old boys who are in the Cub Scouts of the Boy Scouts of America.

You have looked over the material that is issued to you to teach to the group. You notice as you are teaching this material that your students are not very open-minded, "Think outside the box," and don't know much about common sense or how to be aware of their surroundings. They just sit there waiting for you to answer the question you previously asked them.

"Why is this?" You quickly realize the answer. They have been taught very little how to think of themselves! You would think that these boys would have been taught this at home. Possibly. This most likely did not happen because their parents did not teach this. Therefore, the parents cannot teach their children what they themselves do not know. You would figure that this is what school is all about. So you send your child to school so that they can be taught things you should know but don't know. Sadly enough, this knowledge is not as fluently taught as you would like it to be. Test this yourself thereof. Ask yourself just what does the school teach your child?

As the den leader, you decide to add this knowledge into the assigned material that you are supposed to teach these nine-to-eleven-year-old boys. You start in showing and speaking respect. You teach them it is "YES, SIR" and "NO, SIR." Also, it is "YES, SIR," and "NO, SIR," to you. Next you inform your students that every time you ask them question, you are not going to give them the answer. No, you are going to ask each and every one personally to give a verbal answer as to what they "think" the answer may be!

All of a sudden, it's very quiet. You notice how big their eyes start getting on the faces of these students. Their mouths start falling open followed by a big gulp, and swallowing a lump on their throat. Now you let them know that they need to pay attention. Also, try not to say the exact same answer that someone sitting next to them already said. You watch the boys start squirming in their seats. By the look in their faces, you don't think you really want to be in this group. Looking around the room "thinking," *Hey, that group over there is really quiet. They don't look like they're doing anything. I think I need to move over to that group.*

So you start by asking the question, "Why did you join the Boy Scouts? Let's start with you, Terry." There is a look of startle on his face. "Don't be afraid to talk, Terry." He has a big gulp followed by silence. "I have a question. Are you afraid to ask your mother if you can have a piece of cake that she just made for the family?"

"No, sir."

"All right, then. There is no need to be afraid of your classmate or to me or to answer the question I have just asked you because after you, I am going to ask each and every one of the group the same question.

"So let's see who is afraid and who is not. Now, Terry, tell the class why you joined the Boy Scouts." Terry looks at you then the rest of the class with this scared "okay" look on his face then verbally gives his answer.

"Very good, Terry. That was not so hard after all. Very good! Now, Bobby." Bobby gives his answer. Then you ask the next boy then the next. They all give their verbal answers to the class. It is really nice to see smiles on all their faces as they think out and feel and show self-confidence of achievement. You appraise them and tell them that you are proud of them for showing courage and that they are fine young men because they are learning to think and speak for themselves. You notice their faces glow with excitement with a smile and sparkling eyes to follow. Now the night is close to the end.

"So next week, we will cover a new topic. So be ready to give an answer to the question because I will be calling on each and every one of you to give your own answer." Before the night is over, you notice one boy. He looks like he is lost. You go over to the young man. "How are you doing, Joe?" He slowly looks up with an unsure look on his face.

"Fine, sir."

"You had a great answer."

"Thank you, sir."

"I will see you next week, right?" You notice an interested look on his face, but you can also sense fear.

"I think so, sir." He has a smile on his face.

"Joe, would you like to learn a whole bunch of things that other boys and girls don't know?"

With a curious, light facial expression, he replies, "Yes, sir, but I am afraid, sir."

"I will teach you how to not be afraid but cautious, okay?"

With a touch of excitement, he replies, "Yes, sir."

"Now I will see you next week, okay?"

"Yes, sir." It is so nice to see the smile on his face.

The next meeting, I give all the boys homework that consists of four quotes. I ask them to write an answer they think it meant. Now we go over some other quotes in class, so they would be able to do their homework with ease. "If you need help, ask your parents, but write the answer in your own words." All the boys are excited.

The following week, they turn in their homework. Most of them have no problem. Joe is not turning in his paper. So you go over to talk to Joe. He sees you coming over to him. He is pretty upset and embarrassed. "Hello, Joe."

Becoming more emotional following silence, with tears in his eyes, he says "I am stupid and an idiot" with a red face and eyes full of tears.

"Why do you think that?"

With tears falling from his eyes, he replies, "Because I am failing school! I am afraid of getting everything wrong. Then everyone gets mad at me, sir."

"What about your parents? Did you ask them for help?"

In a soft voice, he says, "No, sir."

Looking into his eyes, you hold a proud smile on your face. "Well, why don't you take this home and ask your parents and relatives for their answers, then write your answers using their answers as a guideline."

"What is a guideline, sir?"

"Something to follow."

"Yes, sir."

"Because here, there is no wrong answer. This is just a game. If you don't want to try, I mean try and play, then yes, you lose or become the loser. Now if you put forth the effort and try to win by playing, you are a winner because you put forth courage and tried. Joe wiped his tears running down his face."

"Yes, sir."

We both notice the rest of the class staring, giggling, and laughing at Joe. This makes a good but unexpected topic to cover. "Now, class, the topic tonight, we are going to talk about hearsay and assumption. You explain and talk with the class that you really need to know the whole story before you start making actions, comments, or try to tell the story to someone else. This is known as gossip. Gossip is something astray that by the time the story comes around full circle, it is not about the whole point. Things get changed that are not fully true. Here, Joe is set and determined to better himself like you. He is going to achieve very high goals. There have been times when all of you wanted to accomplish something, but it seems there was always something in the way that is keeping you from accomplishing your goal. I will help you learn how to remove whatever is in your path that you consider as a blockage. Now I am going to ask each one of you to tell the class of your own experience as to when this happened to you."

The look on their faces are priceless. They all give their stories. Now you point out there is no reason to laugh at Joe. They all well understand with respect.

The following class, Joe gives you his homework. Boy is glowing as he told you, "Thank you. Now I understand, sir. I might be just above failing now, but soon, I will be a straight-*A* student."

"Joe, yes, you can. Yes, you will reach your goal. I am proud of you as you are appraising. Joe—" his face glows even brighter with a smile a mile wide and with sparkling eyes—"Joe."

"Yes, sir."

"Do you have a plan to go by to accomplish your straight-*A* goal?" Joe's face slowly dense down.

"Sir, I do not know what you mean. A plan?"

"Yes, Joe. You may have a goal to reach, but you need a plan to be put together, so you will have a guideline to follow."

"Mr. M. Sir, will you help me build a plan?" His face lights up exciting interest.

"Why, yes, sir Joe. I need you to take a piece of paper and pen. I am going to help you make a list of things to follow that will accomplish your goal, ready?"

"Yes, sir."

"Number one: go talk to your teacher, and let them know you are striving to accomplish this goal. Write this down."

"Oh, yes, sir. How do you spell *s-t-r-i-v-i-n-g*?"

"Okay, next. Number two: do your homework. Don't play video games. You play them after your homework is done."

"Yes, sir."

"Number three: ask for extra credit work."

"Yes, sir."

"Number four: read a chapter in advance of the class. This way, you will already be prepared for the topic when the teacher talks about it."

"Yes, sir."

"Number five: if you don't understand something, make sure you ask your teacher to help you understand. Now let me know if you have any questions."

"Yes, sir."

"Now this is called a layout plan. If you follow it, it will lead you to your goal." You look at Joe with a smile, and he raises his eyebrows. It's that simple. "Got any questions?"

With a funny wide smile and large sparkling eyes, he replies, "No, sir, not at this time. Thank you, sir."

As the year goes by, Joe shows you his report card with pride. Yes, each time he does, his grades move up a letter. Soon, all the boys are showing you their report cards with pride. Yes, all their grades are coming up fast.

At the end of the school year, guess what? That's right. Joe shows you his last report card. Yes, he had all *A*s on it. He is glowing like a beacon as he told you "Thank you" with tears in his eyes for all you have done. The two of you share a firm handshake. All of a sudden, Joe lunges forward and wraps his arms around your waist. "Thank you, sir," he says in a crackled gentle voice. You finally part as you notice Joe wiping his tears as he smiled.

"You're welcome, Joe," you says as you try to hold back the moisture in your eyes due to the whole situation.

"Now I am going to be a college graduate."

"I am very proud of you, Joe. You have come a long way. You have set your goals and achieved them. I am impressed at your success. As a suggestion, maybe your next goal is to be the top of your class all through high school. Then the goal of a college top graduate will be easier to accomplish."

"Yes, sir. Thank you, sir," he says while holding the biggest smile with sparkling eyes.

Do your Home Work: Get a second opinion: Do your research: Compare your options: Do you have a plan?

The Chalkboard
Did you pass the mind reading class?

You never really miss seeing a chalkboard until you need one. Early in the year, you can talk and describe to your students what something looked like but you know that what you see is not exactly what they envision.

Therefore, you know the only way everyone can be on the same page of thinking as you is to be seeing the same thing or a chalkboard. Problem number one: the building you are meeting in does not have a chalkboard.

To solve this problem, you can use your eraser board. In order to accomplish the goal of teaching, this is improvised.

Do your Home Work: Get a second opinion: Do your research: Compare your options: Do you have a plan?

Be Aware of Your Surrounding
Learning to observe

The material that you are issued to teach in the book teaches the Cub and Boy Scout that where there is a large body of water, someone drowns. The contents in this book describe that if you come up on someone who is drowning, example, a lake, you are to look and find a ten-foot stick. You are to use this to rescue the drowning person. Do not get in the water! So you view this logical common sense. One: what are the chances that you are going to find a ten-foot stick in time? Two: what if the drowning person is twenty feet or more from the shoreline? Three: you are not to get in the water!

This is what you are issued to teach! Now what if this is your son or daughter in the water screaming to the top of their lungs in fear trying to get someone's attention for help? Now what if there is a Cub or Boy Scout present, what do you think your son's or daughter's chances are to be rescued? Now you know that if you teach these kids to be aware of their surroundings, you could save a life. You figured the best logical common sense way is to take your eraser board and to the next class.

When class starts, you inform the group that tonight's topic is to be "aware of your surroundings." This class tonight may save someone else's life, maybe your own. "Class, here on this board, I am going to draw many things." You should have seen the surprised, excited look on their faces as you are setting up the board.

"Now we will talk about the picture I have drawn. Now you draw a lake and lakeshore. There is a flat bottom boat that is resting on the shore. There is a fishing rod and reel that someone used to catch fish with inside the boat that you can see. There is a life jacket hanging over the side of the boat. There is an empty plastic water bottle and an empty milk jug lying on the ground next to the boat. There is a burnt-out campfire close to the boat. There is a pedestrian about a half a block away. Yes, in the picture, there is someone in the lake not far from shore who is trashing and screaming to the top of their lungs in fear of drowning."

You ask each boy what do they see in the picture. Mostly, the answer is someone drowning. Is this an answer of emotion and sorrow? "Now, fellows, you need to think with logic." You ask them one at a time to look at the picture and find something or some way you can use or do to save the person who is drowning. You cannot get in the water. You only have seconds to respond.

"Next question: How far out from the shore is the drowning person?" All the boys said it looks like more than ten feet. You use the wall behind them to show it is eight feet tall as a reference to ten feet. "Did all of you notice the burnt-out campfire? So what are the chances you are going to find a ten-foot stick lying around?"

They said none.

"Fellows, this is a practice drill. One day, this may happen to you. From what you learn here tonight, you can save a life, maybe your friend. Now look at the picture again. Find something in the picture you can substitute for a ten-foot stick. Now use our imagination. The ten-foot stick rule is gone. There are no rules, except do not get in the water and after them because you are not trained to do so." You ask the boys one at a time. They all have a different answers. They say they could do the following:

1. Push the boat out to them, then paddle it to them.
2. Throw them the life jacket that is in the boat.
3. Throw them the milk jug lying beside the boat.
4. Holler for help to the pedestrian.
5. Tie the water bottle on to the fishing line of the rod and reel, then cast the bottle to the drowning person, then reel them in.

You appraise all the boys for their thoughts and answers. Now you address each answer to see which of the answers would be most practical. For example, could you throw the life jacket or the milk jug the distance needed and hit the target? It is really nice to watch their faces and listen to them talk about how to handle the situation which showed the boys were really thinking for themselves.

Do your Home Work: Get a second opinion: Do your research: Compare your options: Do you have a plan?

The Camping Trip at the Lake
Improvising

My group of boys in the pack are headed to a destination at which we will be camping next to a lake. We all arrived and got tents set up. While setting around the campfire, the boys were asking if they can go swimming and do some fishing. "Boys, you know we have work to do, then we can, but the ones who will get in the water, I need to know. Can all of you swim?" All of a sudden, I just hear, "I can, I can." I know there is always one—the one that said "I can," but they know they cannot!

The next day, we did committee service for the park. Then the following day, we rested and sat around the campfire because it was chilly. One day, looking at the pretty sunrise, the boys wanted to go fishing on the pier while the other boys wanted to swim. The parents who went as chaperones were getting prepared to walk over to the shoreline to assist and watch the boys play in the water. Due to the impeccant excitement of going swimming, the boys all of a sudden, took off running for the water. I hollered, "You can only get in the water waist-deep because I don't know who can actually swim and who cannot."

Now do you think in a time like this all the boys listened to you? Yes, you are right. There is always one!

One of the boys got out too far. There was a drop-off ledge. This boy didn't not know how to swim. The screaming started. You saw the splashing. You were stripping your shoes and wallet as you run for the water to rescue the boy. All of a sudden, everyone was hollering, "Look, Terry is pulling Bobby in with his fishing pole."

Terry had large bobbers in his line while fishing from the pier. That is what Bobby grabbed as Terry casted him his line. Then Terry reeled Bobby to shallow water. This was one unique fishing trip for Terry, saving a life by landing a real-live person with his fishing rod and reel.

Do your Home Work: Get a second opinion: Do your research: Compare your options: Do you have a plan?

The Walking Stick or Staff

This piece of wood can be your best friend and can also save your life. When you took this job to teach young boys, you really took on a large responsibility because you want to be sure of their safety at all times and prepare them for what is ahead in life. Using logical common sense, now you know that there are going to be a lot of camping trips that will include hiking. When in the wilderness, you need to be aware of the unexpected to happen at any moment. So here, you decide to discuss in the next class the topic of "how a staff can be your best friend" and save someone or your life. Here, you decide to buy closet rods that are ten-feet long then cut them in half, so you have the correct number for each student plus one for yourself. Then you go to a local pet store where you can buy a real-looking rubber snake.

Now it is time to load up all these materials and head to the location where everyone meets for class. Try to imagine the looks that you got from everyone in the building as you carry in this bundle of sticks. Yes, a lot of big eyes and jaws are dropping. All of your boys are surprised. "Now tonight, this is the topic that we are going to cover. This, as you see it, a wooden stick, but another name it is called a staff." So you ask the boys, "How many things can this wooden staff be used for?"

It is very impressive to hear the boys come up with such a wide variety of answers. "You know, fellows, everyone is thinking and thinking outside the box. All of you gave fantastic answers. All of you are correct with your answers. Now there is one thing that no one said. That is what we are going to talk about. Also, we are going to practice." The look in their faces are "Wow, wow!" They have sparkling eyes and big smiles of excitement. The boys are very excited even though they do not know what we're going to practice. They just know we are going to do something exciting.

What the group practiced is walking in twos formation—one looking straight ahead while the other is watching down the path to see where to step. Then they would change places or look out. We use the rubber snake many times. For example, how one would see the snake and use the staff and keep the other boy from stepping on it. We do this exercise because of future trail hikes we are planning to attend. The walking staff have many ways to assist the walker.

Do your Home Work: Get a second opinion: Do your research: Compare your options: Do you have a plan?

The Hotlist Camping Trip
Courage-Honor

Here it is, the middle of summer. There is a high-pressure system that has been setting over the state for the past month. No rain in the past or insight. Cities are starting to ration water. The Boy Scout pack is scheduled to camp for the weekend at a regular park. When the pack arrives, everyone is informed that you cannot drive your vehicle to the campsite because there is tall dry grass. There have been cases that an exhaust system on a vehicle has started grass fires. Therefore, everyone will have to hand pack all of their camping supplies to their assigned campsite. Once, we have packed in our supplies then set up our tents. Generally, we have a campfire to sit around that evening. Due to the burn band, we cannot have a campfire. This is heartbreaking tradition. One of the best things about camping is sitting around a campfire and getting smoke in your eyes as you roast marshmallows. One nice thing about it being so hot is there are no mosquitoes.

After the sun went down and is getting late, everyone is waiting for the temperature to cool down to turn in for some sleep. Did I say sleep? The temperature is still in the high eighties, eighty-seven degrees. Try to lay on air mattress and have sweat rolling down your sides, face, and legs. Soon, you have realized you are lying in a puddle of sweat as it accumulates on your air mattress. Do you think you can fall asleep during all this? This went on for hours 'til about 3:00 a.m.

You get off your air mattress, rise up one end to drain off all the sweat it has accumulated, and then it finally cooled down enough, so you can doze off. As soon as the sun comes up, it does not take long to feel the heat again. So now you are tired and tries not to be grumpy. Your group, as well as the rest of the group, heads for the small lake, so they can take turns paddling in canoes. Along the way, there are different parents who went as chaperones. They will ask you in a humorous, mocking way of disapproval. "Why does your group carry those sticks and the other group do not?"

You explain with a tired, stun look, walking in the wilderness on these trips.

"There is no telling what you will walk up on. For example, the biggest concern is snakes. Walking in or on wilderness trails is not the same as walking on a concert sidewalk in the city. I take you have only walked in the city." Silence. They look at each other then you.

"Well, we did not think about that!"

After the group finished with the canoe exercise, the group gather together, so we can hike back to camp for lunch then we will go to the next exercise. The path to camp that we were going to go down is dense. The foliage is somewhat thick. The grass is well up to knee-deep for the boys. This trail is very narrow. Now you instruct the boys to single file behind you. You want to take point because you are concerned for the safety of your group. So you start down the narrow high grass with foliage blocking the view of the trail.

You let everyone know to use your sticks as a friend on this trail. You start walking point. All of a sudden, to your right is a young Cub Scout walking in a two-man group formation. You tell him to walk behind you, but for some reason, the young boy does not respond to your request. With a stern, serious look on his face and tone of voice, he says "No, sir. I need to walk beside you" with the biggest smile on his face.

"What do you do?" After all, you trained these boys to walk in a pair.

"Sir, like you said in the exercise, one looks ahead while the other watches the path." I look at the young man.

"Yes, sir, young man. Shall we proceed?"

"Yes, sir." Here, you are tired hungry walking along. You hear your stomach rumbling. Everything else is fine. You are constantly looking back behind you to see the rest of the group is safe right behind you. You hear someone says, "Look!"

You are looking all around as the boys behind you are talking, but you don't see what someone said look. You are trying to figure out what you are supposed to see.

All of a sudden, you feel this most excruciating pain right across your right shin bone. You just stop. Don't move. Responding to this intense pain, you want to scream it hurts so badly; but because you are the strong one and you are the leader, you just bite your tongue and muffle your scream. Then you look down at your leg where the extreme pain is to see a walking stick laid across your shin. With eyebrows down, a painful made look on your face, you have your eyes start at your shin, and follow the stick to find it ends in the hands of the young man that has been walking beside you. You follow from the hand up to the face. Now you are looking at the serious smiling face of the young Cub Scout as he points downward about sixteen inches in front of you on the path. With your eyebrows down, your eyes follow his pointed finger. Woo! Your eyebrows bounce upward. Your eyes widen, bring into focus, and you see a very large light-brown or copper-colored coiled up copperhead snake in the striking position. You swallow a large lump in your throat, realizing the next step you would have taken. You would have stepped on this snake and got bitten. Very slowly, you tell the young Cub Scout that both of you will move back very slowly. The whole time, the snake is ready to strike. After catching a great of relief thinking for the safety of the rest of the group, you use your walking stick to politely encourage the large copperhead snake that he needs to slide away quickly, so you may pass.

Everyone hears the word *snake*. A commotion starts. "Quiet. Now, boys, use your walking stick to beat the grass. All the way to the end of the trail."

Once you reach the end of the trail, you got the color back on your face. You go over to the young man that saved you from stepping on that snake and getting snake bite.

"Robert, I cannot thank you enough for what you did for me."

"Thank the Lord above."

"Thank you, Robert."

"You're welcome, sir. I cannot say thank you enough for all that you have taught me, sir."

"How about a handshake?"

"Yes, sir." Our hands come together. You could feel the very firm grip of this young man. The handshake continues longer than normal. After we shake hands, you notice that both of us have collected a little moisture in our eyes.

The Elementary School Teacher

During the school year, there was a teacher who had several of my students in her class. One day, while taking my son to school, I am notified by one of the other teachers that Ms. N would very much like to talk to me. She said it is very important. Okay, I will wait. The first thought that goes through my mind is, *Oh, no! Is my son in trouble?*

Suddenly, *Oh, there is Ms. N.* She is hurrying down the hall, waving her hands at me with a big smile on her face. As she gives me hand signals, she says, "Just a minute. I will be right there." I nod with a smile of understanding. Oh, here she comes in a hurry in a Tiptoe fashion with a big smile on her face. Her hands pointed right for me as she gets very close to me. I see her hands come together and she places them on her chest with a very radiant smile following southern tone of voice and facial body expression.

"Oh, Mr. M, how are you doing this morning?"

"Just fine, and you?"

"Oh, my. I would like to talk and ask you if you help me understand something as well as how to overcome this tense little problem I am dealing with. Please, please, if you don't mind."

The first thought that goes through my mind, *Does this teacher have students she held back a year?*

"Why? Ms. N, is my son in trouble?"

"Oh, no, Mr. M. This is not about your son. This is about…are you a den leader for the Boy Scouts?"

"Yes, ma'am. I am.

"Well, you see, I have several boys in my class that you have in your class. Okay. Well, that is what I want to talk to you about," she says as she graciously moves her body and hands toward you then pulls her hands back together in front of her chest. She then rests her palms flat on her chest with this bright smile and sparkling eyes.

"Okay, go on. What is it you want to discuss?" You notice her bright smile, battering eyelashes, and face glow. All of a sudden, her facial expression changes to a low tone.

"Well, you see, Mr. M, these boys, at the beginning of the year, were very quiet. They would not really participate in class discussions."

She stops and looks at me with a concerned, troubled look on her face.

"Okay, what is your point?"

Now the facial expression really turns to a serious look. "Mr. M, I am not used to it."

"What are you talking about?"

"These boys have done 180 degrees turn around. They are very much participating in class. They come up with the most thoughtful answers. Their grades are coming up. They are giving answers to questions that I should know, but I don't know. So how is it these nine-to-eleven-year-old boys that you are teaching know so much?" She asks with a stern facial expression and points finger right at you. "Look, I am the teacher, and they are the students! I do not like the circumstances of what is going on at this stage of my teaching career!" She has this detective look on my face.

"Well, I am going to ask you a question. I do not intend to offend you, but I am going to ask the question, okay?" The look you get from her is possibly fear or anger. She stands there and says nothing. "Do you want me to ask you the question or not?" The look on her face now lightens with a color and curiosity.

"Okay, you can ask me."

"Well, thank you. Do you feel intimidated by these boys?"

With a deep breath, she looks at me like "How dare you!" as she just stands there staring at me with cold, dark eyes. I am trying to hide the smile I would like to display. "I am waiting for an answer."

With a distrait facial expression followed by a very sad puppy-dog-eyed expression, I think I see moisture accumulating in her eyes as she places a napkin to each eye.

"Okay, yes."

"You see the situation, and you do not like it. Are the students teaching the teacher?" I ask with raised eyebrows. There is total silence. What a mad look with a cold, dark eye on her facial expression as I raise my eyebrows and smile. I notice a very stern voice and body posture as she points her finger right at me.

"Look, Mr. M. I am the teacher, and they are the students! That is and how it will always be!" With a slight stomp trying to hold back a smile, I know that I am fixing to get reprimanded, prosecuted, or chewed out for teaching. What is the use to being tough in schools? So I hunker down and get ready to launch a counter defense.

With a stern but polite posture and tone of voice, I say, "Look, Ms. N. As I see it, you are perturbed at me for teaching what I teach."

With a loud voice and showing of anger, she replies "That's right, Mr. M. This is all your doing!" while looking at her pointed finger real close to my chest.

With a slight smile on my face and relaxed tone of voice, I say, "Well, Ms. N, you are really showing your true colors."

With a stepped up stern tone of voice, I say, "Now let me bring this to your attention. If you have any qualms about this, you do not take it out on the students because if you do, you and I will pay administration a visit! You do not take it out on me. You need to take it up with the school board or higher! Why, you did not get taught this in any school you were in. Now your jealousy is only discrediting you and your teacher profile."

With a firm, stern tone of voice, I say "Do you understand?" followed by a stern, cold-eye look. With a polite comical smile, I ask, "Do you have any more questions or points you want to discuss?" I see the facial look of "I am sorry."

"Mr. M, I am so sorry for my actions and blaming you for something I should have never done. I am truly sorry."

"Okay. You mean that this used to be taught in school? I see you must have learned the same."

"Well, you know now that I think about it. They did not teach any of this for as long as I can remember. I offer my apology to you, Mr. M."

"Okay, apology accepted."

During the whole time of this discussion, there have been a continuous number of teachers' heads looking around the corner watching us having our discussion in the hall of the school while using from time to time a loud voice. "Mr. M, I don't blame you if you say no due to my actions, but I am going to ask you this question."

"What is the question?"

With this glamor facial expression, she asks, "Will you explain to me your teaching style? So I can enhance my performance as a teacher. Also, it is very important I stay one step ahead of my students. Instead of right now, I am one step behind the students. Please." She pulls her hands together in a praying form.

Logically thinking, I will be helping the students, the teacher, and future students. She stands in front of me with this look of mercy holding her hand in praying form. "Please, please! Oh, please."

"Yes, I will help you. Teach you roughly the type of teaching I do."

"Oh, thank you, Mr. M."

We spent roughly an hour together going over this information. As the time is to part ways, I see the respect, gratitude, and thankfulness in her facial expression.

"Oh, thank you so much, Mr. M" as she shows in body language.

Then she asks, "Would you like to share a hug to cap the ordeal?" I look at her smile. I smile certainly with open arms. The two of us come together and embrace each other. She is rubbing her hands on my back. She is polite, so I do the same. Suddenly, I feel she intensifies the hug. I can feel her body pressing against mine. Then the holding tension of the arms start to relax. She then gently gives me a soft kiss on the right cheek of my face. As the two of us separates, she says, "Thank you, Mr. M."

"You're welcome, Ms. N."

The year goes by. I find there is little to no further conversations. I do notice when I am in sight, she smiles and gives me two thumbs-up hand signal. I just have to nod and smile followed by a wave of hand. The year comes to a close. It is graduation time. Here, I see my son and all of his classmates get recognized for graduating to the next grade level.

Then the teachers are recognized for their performance. What a coincidence! Ms. N is handed a large plaque then announced the Teacher of the Year award.

Do your Home Work: Get a second opinion: Do your research: Compare your options: Do you have a plan?

Open House

As a parent, you remember all the times you went to the schools to meet the teachers that your child will have during the school year.

This year, you go with your son to the high school he will be attending this year. There, you will meet a lot of faculty. While you were there, you wanted to meet a teacher. You heard she was teaching team leadership.

The information you heard was she was fantastic. Her students were very ecstatic due to what she was teaching and due to what they were learning. So you ask around to find this popular teacher, so you can get a chance to meet her. Finally some other faculty member points to this well-dressed woman who is talking to, possibly, parents. You make your own way to the area of where the woman is standing, waiting for your turn to introduce yourself and speak with her. The other people she is talking to leave with a parting handshake. She looks at you with the prettiest smile and sparkling eyes. You notice not only the pretty smile and sparkling eyes but a glow in her facial expression. Then she turns to you. "How can I help you?" She reaches out her hand for an introduction handshake.

"How are you, ma'am?"

"Just fine." Her smile grows larger.

"Yes, ma'am. Do you teach team leadership here at the high school because I have heard such fantastic results." Her face brightens with a beautiful smile.

"Well, yes, sir. I do."

"I have heard that you are a fantastic teacher and that your students are really progressing from what you are teaching."

"Oh, yes! My students just love the material I am using in class! My students have really brought up all their grades." You both talk about the higher success they have. "Now how can I help you?"

"Yes, ma'am. The information I heard you are using is from a poster of quotes that came from a faculty member of the elementary school." Like slow motion, her beautiful smile slowly fades, and her sparkling eyes went cold. With an energetic smile, you say, "Ma'am, I am asking you. We can help each other!"

"Sir, what are you asking of me?" She pulls her hands up to her chest.

"Would you write me a letter addressing the enjoyment and the progress of your students at which you have just described? I will help you with more of this information and style. You see, I introduced this material to the elementary faculty last year that you are using."

With a straight face and a very concerned tone of voice, she says, "Sir, I don't follow what you are getting at!"

"This information you are using is great. Even the faculty of the elementary took a very high interest liking to it. I am asking you to help me prove its importance to the students by enhancing their life as they go through life."

The wonderful teacher stands there, blank look on her face, and speechless. Then politely, she says, "Sir, will you excuse me? I have a lot of people to meet and to talk to."

"Yes, ma'am. It has been a pleasure."

She has already turned and walked away.

Do your Home Work: Get a second opinion: Do your research: Compare your options: Do you have a plan?

The Unexpected

Intimation—a frown with lowered eyebrows is often an intention of disapproval.

Jealous—full of envy; envious. He is jealous of John or of John's marks.

Insecure—a region when life is insecure.

The information that I have covered in this book was taught to me by my grandfather and my aunt who later become my adopted second mother. This book is in dedication to both of them and others.

As a young lad, I had reached the age that I would have to start school. I was given an evaluation test to see where the best place to start: preschool or the first grade.

After I took the test, the person giving the test told my parents they need to put me in a private school. The reason why is because I am advanced. I will fail in public school due to boredom.

My first day of school was a nightmare to me. I was used to staying home and playing on the farm helping out chores with my aunt. Soon, I overcome the change. Now I played marbles with the other kids.

By the time of the fourth grade, we were covering the sixth grade public school information. The fifth grade is when I started public school. One thing I learned was a lot of teachers who taught private schools had moved to teach in public schools. I came to find out my fifth grade teacher was one of these teachers. I thought this was really neat.

We all can remember one or more teachers that we had in school that made such an everlasting impression that really helped shape our lives. In my opinion, she was fantastic. She was an assume teacher I will always remember with admiration.

One day, she said, "Class, each one of you are going to pick a president you like. Then do a research on the president before. Then after, you will be writing a report. Today it is called an essay on the presidents. In your report, tell why and what good this president did for our country. Then include in your report out of the three presidents who was the best for our country; who was the worst."

She gave us hints as to where we could find the information. Then she informed us to have parents proofread your report so that "you can present a very nicely, neat handwritten report." This will be displayed at open house one month from today.

There is always one. There was a student who was afraid to ask their parents for assistance or help. Why? Maybe you can figure this out?

Ask yourself were you ever afraid to ask your parents for help? Anyway, the student asked someone else to help them with their report.

The night of open house, it was really neat to watch the parents smile and see them raise their eyebrows and glow with admiration then tell the teacher how delighted and impressed they were for what she had done—the most fantastic job in teaching her students by seeing the displays on the floor.

Each student gave the presentations, especially how unique the nicely, neat handwritten reports that the students have done. All of a sudden, out of nowhere, this parent starts bursting out as she speaks. She gets louder and louder! "Oh, my word! Oh, my word! Oh, my word! I cannot believe you are making my child and these fifth-grade students to write an essay that is equal to a college freshman level. This is absurd!"

Very loudly, she is steady chewing out the teacher up one side and down the other. She was trashing her hands and stomping her feet. Her facial expression looked like she had just been given a big fat *F* on a major school project while her child was given a 100 on their major school project. Here, showing her jealousy there in public in front of all the other parents was just unbelievable. In a very upset voice, moisture collecting her eyes, she was yelling out, "I was never taught any of this when I was in fifth grade."

With leaning forward body posture, her hands extended far from her sides, and her facial expression of emotional disgrace.

"Why are you teaching my child this?" Tears were rolling down her very emotionally angry face.

It was so sad to see the radiant glow, the beautiful smile, and the sparkling eyes of pride of her student that my teacher held on her facial expression then watch all of this on my teacher's face just melted away down to tears.

This all happened so quickly. Everyone was in shock. This was unbelievable. With a stern posture, very stern voice, and good manners, I was not going to stand and watch this continue! I walked over to the woman.

"Ma'am, as far as I am concerned, my teacher is one of the most assume teacher I have ever had. She is helping us kids get an early start on the real world. Just because you were not taught this during your time of school years, you need to take your frustration, your actions of jealousy, and complaints out on the people in the capital who run the school. Not this teacher! Now I am going to ask you to apologize to my teacher. Then you need to leave this building because I will go and get someone to escort you out of here, ma'am."

She just stood there with a shocked look on her face only to see all of other parents were staring at her with dark eyes and eyebrows down.

I turned to look at my teacher. She was catching moisture from the corner of her eyes with a tissue and slightly shaking her head up and down with a smile on her face, sparkling eyes, showing her admiration. The rest of the parents were in an awe! Then they all just looked back at the woman. Their facial expression was now "you have to apologize to this teacher before you leave this room." They all started to move toward her. The woman turned with a scared look on her face and made a quick apology to my teacher. Then hurried very quickly out of the classroom. Unbelievable.

The next day, she did give my teacher a long apology then went to the principal to constantly complain. Unbelievable.

All through my years of school, elementary, junior high school, high school, and even college, I have watched as the principal or dean pull the teacher out of the middle of class to stand in the hall right in front of the classroom door with glass, use a stern posture, eyebrows down to their nose, and very stern tone of voice. They would drive their point finger into the chest of the teacher, telling them if they do not stop teaching information like this in this book, they are going to get fired or they need to resign. "Do you understand?" Unbelievable.

Some teachers stood their grounds. This still goes on today! Why are parents sending their kids to private school? Why are parents homeschooling their children? As a parent, are you going to hold your child back? As a parent, are you going to do everything you can to give your child a very solid foundation which will prepare them for issues in society?

Do your Home Work: Get a second opinion: Do your research: Compare your options: Do you have a plan?

The Romantic Dinner

You really love your wife with respect and honor. You, at times, when the two of you are in public places, you feel like you are her bodyguard because of all the crime that takes place in the real world. Things generally happen when you least expect it. This unexpected event can turn your life upside down, become tragic, or even fatal.

When she is going to places, for example, to work or shopping malls, you find yourself calling her on the phone not only to hear her sweet, lovely voice but also to check on her well-being and safety. By just telling her how much you loved her, you are concerned of her well-being.

When you think about it, you are a fortunate guy because your wife is a blessing. The things that she does for you and your family. She will go out of her way to do all. She puts the family first.

When the two of you are together, you let her know how much you appreciate her thoughtfulness, kindness, and consideration.

This is when you just hold her in your arms looking at her sweet smile and sparkling eyes as you let her know that she is one very beautiful woman who is very unique in her own way.

"Thank you for being my wife."

You notice how her face glows and tears of joy start filling her eyes. Hearing her soft voice saying "Thank you" as she raises up on her toes to kiss you on your lips, you feel a very intense hug she shares with you. You know this is very important in her life because she has sensitive feelings. Sometimes it gets very emotional.

It is your wedding anniversary. Just think about it. You and that wonderful woman have been married for all those great years.

So you make reservations at the new, very nice restaurant that has opened up on the edge of town there on the edge of waterfront property overlooking the lake. You have done your research. They serve a fantastic steak and seafood plus a buffet with a very polite courteous staff and roll-up parking.

This is really going to surprise and impress her to dine in the evening while viewing the night-lights, reflecting on the water of the lake while you sit there sharing a candle flicker flame while sipping on some Sharna white wine.

You made the reservations for Saturday night. You walk through the front door of your house Friday afternoon from a good day's work. You see your beautiful wife standing in the kitchen, preparing supper. You quietly walk up behind her. She lightly turns her head. You notice a happy facial expression. You open your arms, slide your hands together as you intensify the squeezing of your arms around her lower chest then very smoothly tilt your head then kiss her on her neck then up to her cheek. You notice her body temperature rising and her heartbeat racing. She starts to turn around. You relax your arms. She turns around in your arms, puts her arms up on your shoulders with this sensitive smile and sparkling eyes. She leans her head forward and presses her lips onto yours. "Well, hello, sweetheart. How was your day?"

"Um, it was okay." Eyebrows up, a smile on your face. "Coming home to you is the best part of the day, baby."

"Well, thank you." It is followed by a second kiss.

"You're welcome." You can see the slight red blush in her face showing pride, appreciation, and the feeling of security.

"Baby, tomorrow night, I am going to take you to a fantastic restaurant for our wedding anniversary. The reservations are for 7:00 p.m."

"Sweetheart, you remembered!"

"Baby, you bet. Married to a fantastic woman like yourself, how can I forget? She just glows with this huge smile and sparkling eyes then bounces on her feet toward the cook top.

"Supper is almost ready."

"Great! Did I ever tell you you are a fabulous cook?"

"You have told me before, but I always like to hear it from time to time."

Saturday afternoon, the two of you are getting ready for the evening with suspense and excitement. You both shower. You put on your nice pants, socks, shined boots, safari cologne, nice shirt, and a good-looking sport coat.

You're watching your wife get ready for the evening. She is fixing her hair, putting on a light shade of makeup, putting her perfume Vera Wang on, and then see her hold up this very nice-looking dress with a store tag still on it. "Hey, baby, did you buy a new dress?"

"Sweetheart." She looks at you with this innocent facial expression while batting her eyes. "I just happen to be in the store. I saw this dress. It was marked down half the price. This is a very good bargain of a sale. Also, you have to look at the occasion. Yes, I bought this new dress. Do you like it?"

"Yes, baby. It is a nice dress."

"Sweetheart, will you help me with this zipper in the back?"

"Okay, baby." You gently push the zipper to the top of her dress then hook the latch. "There you go, baby."

"Thank you, sweetheart."

"You're welcome."

Then you watch her slide her hands down both sides of the dress pressing out any wrinkles. "Sweetheart—" as she turns her head from side to side—"do I look fat in this dress?"

With your eyebrows up, suspenseful facial expression, and sly smile of concern, you reply, "Baby, I need you to stand up straight, turn a little to the right, lean forward, just a little bit more. Pull your shoulders back—" With your hand holding your chin, shaking your head up and down—"baby, oh my goodness! People's heads are going to turn for you!"

Your eyebrows are up shaking your head up and down and a smile of admiration. "Trust me! Wo!" She shows the feeling of acceptance, beauty, and admiration in her facial expression while holding a smile and sparkling eyes of appreciation.

You drive to the restaurant and park. You hurry to the other side of the car. The door is already open. You stretch out your arm and reach out with your open hand to join with her hand. Then with grace, you assist your wife as she steps out of the car. While holding her hand, both start walking toward the front doors of the entrance. There are people doing the same. *It was nice for my wife to watch people turn and admire us as a couple.*

You both step up to the entrance door. You reach over and grab the door handle. You walk in first then your wife. Now you are turning your head side to side slowly as you are observing the surrounding, looking for anything suspicious because you are the protector. After standing in the lobby, you feel or sense a safe environment. At ease with a smile on your face, you turn to your wife. You are stunned by what you see. Your wife's face is a little red. This is no blush red. Her eyes are cold. There is no smile, only the look of letdown, disappointment, and humility. You're not sure on what to think.

"Baby, are you okay?" She sighs as the look on her face deepens with a mild tone of disgust. "I cannot believe after all the years we have been married, you did not show the decency of holding the door open, so your wife could walk into the restaurant first!" Looking at her facial expression, you can very easily come to the conclusion her emotional feelings were hurt very badly.

While holding a neutral facial expression on your face, you look from side to side only to see the people around you giving you this look of disgust.

"How could you!" You realize the best possible way to handle this. Do not get mad but give a logical explanation. You realize a scene has been started, so you figure on continuing making a good constructive scene, remembering to stay polite, courteous, and constructive not just for your lovely wife but to all the people standing around you in the area.

Using a mild tone of voice and looking directly into the beautiful eyes of your fantastic wife, you say, "Baby, you are 100 percent correct. I should have let you walk through the door first because emotionally, you wanted to be admired like Cinderella as she enters the ballroom. You wanted to see head turns toward you and enjoy the feeling of admiration and acceptance from the people there. That is a sensational feeling. Baby, think about this logically. I love you. My feelings I have is for your concern and happiness, also your safety. In the world today, everyone thinks nothing dangerous will ever happen to them; only to someone else because of my love, care, and concern. Logically, that is why I came in the door first to protect you from any unexpected danger. As I walked in front of you, I am observing our surroundings for your safety and mine. You look from side to side at all the people standing around you. You ask how many of you men observed this area here to check on the safety to where you are satisfied that your wife or date is in a safe place? Or did you just walk in here taking for granted that any and every place is safe from danger because you feel you are invincible or just don't care because it always happens to someone else?" You notice the look on the faces of the men.

"He does have a point."

The look on the faces of the women.

"I did not think about that."

Now you know you just made a huge scene. So with open arms, palms up, eyebrows up, and a funny smile, you look at your wife. "Well, baby, what do you think?" You notice a blush red facial expression with sparkling eyes and a smile of admiration with her shoulders rocking back and forth. "Well, sweetheart, dining at this restaurant, celebrating our anniversary, being married to you, we will have an extraordinary event to remember. Baby, shall we dine?"

You hold your right elbow up. Your wife places her hand on top of your arm as the two of you walk forward. You heard different types of admiration from the people around your wife and you.

Procrastinate versus Logic

Procrastinate—to put off doing something until a future time; to postpone or delay needlessly.

You have the American dream. You want to be very well-educated because you know knowledge is very powerful. You want to be financially independent and wealthy because you know in our society that money is the tool or item of exchange. Therefore, we all need it as much as possible. Now think of all the reasons and write a list. Why have you not achieved the level of knowledge you set a goal for or just wish you had? Now think of all the reasons why you do not have an extra income such as home-based business?

Do you ever wonder why you see other people to be more successful than you see yourself? Do you often wonder how that person is so successful at achieving their knowledge? How is it that person is so successful with their home-based business?

Based on a survey, you may want to do your own survey. It has been proven that the people who are most successful think and work based on logic.

They know that there are steps that have to be completed or done. So they view the situation and check to see if they have overlooked anything. With confidence and satisfaction, they just do it! Then they go to the next step because they have seen the rewards of logical consistency while constantly doing their research on how the system is set up. So they are in step or one step ahead of the game.

Remember when you were in school? Did you read one chapter ahead of schedule? I did. Maybe you did also. Then when the next class was in session, you already knew what was going to be covered plus you were ready and able to discuss the topic with confidence. Then you will prepare for the homework assignment. You may have noticed the professor looks at you, wondering, *How is it you know so much of the material that I have not covered yet?* with amazement. Then when it comes to a major test, you make a very high grade.

They may sometimes think to themselves you have a cheat sheet somewhere. I remember some of my professors in college would make that imply to me. With a smile and confidence and with a high self-esteem, say, "Sir or ma'am, I just did my homework." The only real person stopping you from being successful at whatever goal you set for yourself *is you*!

Logic is the beginning of knowledge.

—James Markham III

Field Tested

When a person reaches adulthood they are very smart in some areas. But they have the tendency to sometimes think that. They have been there, done that, seen that, been around the world twice, and sailed the seven seas once.

While working for a company. There were safety meetings every day in the morning. I was given permission to give presentations covering the material that is in my book. I would discuss emotion vs logic, to a large group standing in a circle. Then I would discuss a quote. I told them that I will be calling on them individually to give a verbal answer as to what you think it means. There is no wrong answer, so don't be afraid to speak. So you people need to pay attention. Because I am going to be calling on you. So do not give the same answers, that the person standing next to you gave. You are going to have to think for yourself. This exercise will improve safety here at this shop or job site. Because you will be more open to see an accident, before it happens. You will be able to stop it before it happens!

Now when I started this information into the safety meetings. Yes you are right! I got a whole lot of MOCKERY! Now I laughed along with everyone else. Then I informed them that I was a den leader for cub-scouts. What I was introducing is the same info, that I am introducing here. I am very proud of those 9-10 year old young men. Because they had developed a mentality of a late teenager. By the end of the year, they were straight A students. Now there are some people here that act like 9-10 year olds. Now if anyone gets offended here what you do as a suggestion. Ask someone you know to video tape you. Without you knowing it. For example, a party. Then view the film at a later time. You will amazed ad what you will see, that you do not see now. Also I am asking you for feedback. Please let me know if this has help you in any way, here or home.

As the weeks went by guys were coming up to me and saying thank you for what you did for me! I would ask? What do you mean. They would with ecstatic answer. I was able to accomplish many things. My family loves this. We are spending more time with laughter and living more harmonious. For example one co worker, said thank you so sincerely. I ask what happened? He said my ex wife and I always are fighting especially when it comes to the kids. I said yes I see your trouble. He said my ex wife and I meet to exchange the kids. There were comments made at first I got so mad. But do to you and your teaching. I was able to stop, caught myself from blurting out, to only make matters worse. I said to myself think! The MISTAKE I almost made, would have been an emotional decision! So I took the time to THINK. I offered a new idea, suggestion, way to handle the issue based on logic. To my ex wife, she stood there with a look of thought. Then said with a pleasant smile, Yes that is a good idea! So we parted both happy agreeing on the new idea.

Now from the beginning of this whole process. The shop superintendent, the welding Foreman, and the women who were representing H.R. they all laughed and showed great MOCKERY. None of these three people like to see coworkers, coming over to me to discuss their progress. And to say thank you. They would say you need to write a book. Because, I sure would buy it!

The employees, began to look forward to the safety meetings. Because of curiosity of what I was going to cover! As time goes by, I overheard the shop superintendent, talking to the welding foreman. Discussing the progress they were making in their life. Example, when they are at the supervisors meetings. How they can make a suggestion, and how all agree to it, then it is final. Plus they have seen such great results at home with their family members. The welding foreman, said yes, I have seen great results with my family. Plus it has enabled me to talk to the workers, in a more productive way, and getting things done. Without squabbling from the the workers. Yes this is pretty nice. My wife asked me, if I had read a book. She did not know of. I said no this comes from a workers, at work. He has introduced this information into our safety meeting. Does he have a book. No he is working on one. Let me know when it is out, so I can buy one. Ok.

One morning the safety meeting was getting under way. ALL of a sudden the shop superintendent burst out into the circle of employees. With his hands high in the air. Hollering stop this! There will be no more of your info presentations, in the safety meetings anymore. I have had it! Now this man is 6 feet plus, that works out a the gym. There I am standing there thinking. This man has just mocked me with humiliation in front of all these coworkers. Now what would you have done if this was you? I asked myself do I get emotional upset? Or do I stand my grounds logically? I could step down and tuck my tail, and blend in with the group. Or logically stand my grounds and confront him. Knowing my name will be placed 1st on the lay off list. So what do you think I did? Your right! Logically I stood my grounds. I turned to him toe to toe, face to face. I informed him in front of the hole group. That took a lot of courage and guts to inform me that you are trying to humiliate me in front of this group by giving this very unprofessional acknowledgement. So now I am going to challenge you, point to the welding foreman, then point to the women representing HR. All three of you have been mocking me this whole time. if this information has helped you here at work, or at home with family in any way at chick I know for a fact this info has helped you! Will you have the same guts and courage to come up to me and apologize and say thank you! Weeks later, all three came to me and apologized with red faces and watery eyes. Then say thank you! Then a week later the shop superintendent asked me if I would come back into the safety meets and continue to present my information

A Moment of Closure

Do you ever wonder why, as a kid, you had a favorite aunt, uncle, or other relative you wanted to be around all the time?

One possible reason for this is that this special person respected you and was very positive and encouraging as they eagerly listened to your conversations and thoughts.

They probably gave you high praise for the things that you had accomplished. Along with that, they likely learned about the things that you hoped to accomplish, and your goals in life.

Maybe they listened and made suggestions for you to think about as you tried to accomplish a little more than they had to do as you worked towards your path that you wanted in your future.

As children, we usually have one set of parents. These parents raised you using the skills-or lack of them, according to the way that they were raised.

Whether it be good or not so good, I was fortunate to have been raised by two sets of parents at the same time. My biological parents would drop me off at a babysitter, my aunt and uncle's house. Over the course of time, I noticed that my aunt and uncle were extremely positive, encouraging and me, whereas my biological parents believed a whole different way.

I later adopted my aunt as my mother as well as my uncle as my father. One day, I asked my aunt why she treated all of us kids like we were guests in her home.

"You treat us with the upmost respect and dignity and encourage so much when it comes to anything and everything we do. Why do you do that?"

She looked at me with a kind of shocked expression on her face. Her eyebrows went up, her head tilted left and she responded, "You know that is a very good question. What we need to do is finish your chores and let me give it some thought. That way, I will be able to answer your question thoroughly."

As we were doing those chores, I notice that she went and talked to her father. She pointed in my direction, then went and talked to her mother. Her hands shook and they flew up into the air when my aunt presented her with the question I had asked. Then, finally, that afternoon, my adopted mom sat down with me and explained it to me in language a youngster would understand.

She put her arms around me and told me that the question I had asked was a very good one.

Curiously, she asked why I had brought the question to her. I looked at her with concern, explaining that I want to learn.

"Why it is that you, my adopted mom and my adopted dad, are so positive encouraging me and the other kids where other relatives are not so positive, encouraging and motivating as you are?" I asked. "Why do you do this?"

She began to tell me that she had set a goal to try to make sure that all of us eight kids learned logic, common sense and creative thinking so we would think outside the box.

That way, she said, we would have a clear view of the path each of us would go down throughout our lifetimes.

She pointed out that we needed to master all of this so that we would be able to see the paths we were going down instead of all the trees that were blocking our view.

We needed to be totally aware of our surroundings at all times, because it is possible for anything to happen when we least expect it and when it does happen, we would know how to approach it in a logical cautious manner. As time went by with this fantastic way of being raised and guided by these parents, I found that the bond between my adopted mother and my father grew so strong that it was totally unbreakable even though everyone has they're not so good points in life.

Because we will always remember the good they did for us, helping us and guiding us down many paths of life that we will go down even though we have not traveled those paths yet.

From being guided and raised in this manner, I was able to accomplish a tremendous amount of goals all through school, knowing that one day I was going to have to go into the real world and make a living.

I would end up getting married, as well as raising a family, and much of this I was taught as a small child came from having two sets of parents.

One set was very positive, encouraging, and motivating; while the other set was the total opposite in many ways. Years passed and I got married, had two girls, then a little boy.

As the years passed, I was constantly telling all of my children that they were very smart and intelligent. I was always strictly positive encouraging and motivating with them, always letting them know that they can do anything if they would just think about what they were going to do before they did it.

Then, I reassured them that they could do it regardless of their ages.

I want to tell you about something that happened to my oldest daughter, and what she learned from the experience.

She asked me to attach a swing to the hook on a swing set. The hook had to be mounted, and was near the top of the swing set.

The kids waited all day long for me to come home from work, to help them. Knowing that I was tired, knowing that I would only take me a few minutes to do this for them, my two daughters asked me if I would attach the hook. I looked at them and asked my oldest why she didn't do it herself. She was surprised looked up at me and explained that she was too small to reach the hook. I told her that just because she was short didn't mean she couldn't get the job done.

I knew it was time for a lesson, so I said we needed to look around the house and yard and find something for her to stand on and use as a ladder. She didn't need a real ladder, just something that would work for the small job.

I explained that it needed to be stable so that she could climb on top of it and reach up and put the hooks and chains where they needed to be. We looked around found a doll highchair on this back patio. We moved it near the swing, set it under where she needed to work and she climbed on top.

I told her to climb up, and she did. Then, I told her to grab both of the rings, hold on to the side of the swing set to brace herself, and put the rings in the holes.

I assured her that I would be standing right there watching her the whole time so that if so that she started to fall, I could catch her.

She said she was not sure she could do the job, but I assured her that she could definitely do it! I told her she needed to plan out the job, and follow through.

I told her to brace herself on the swing set and put the chain on the hook where it needed to go. She climbs up on the high chair and placed one side where it belonged. I told her she had done a good job, and now she needed to get in a good solid position and reach over with one hand and put the other chain on the other hook.

She did as I told her, and turned to me with a surprised look on her face.

She was so astonished, she couldn't believe that she had done it all by herself. And, she was very impressed that I spent the time with her to show her how to carefully plan out what she needed to do-in a very safe manner.

Another example of showing children they can plan a chore and follow it through until it is done was when we got a new bed.

The girls were helping to put the bed rails in place when my almost four old said he wanted to help. He kept asking over and over if he could help.

The girls told him he was too small and too young and would just get in the way.

I stood there and looked at the girls told them there was always a job for everyone.

I told them to let him help, but to remember he was small.

There were some small latches that needed to go on the bed, so he was given the job of picking them up and handing them to us.

I told my son to bring them over and set them in a place where we could reach them.

These slats had to be placed one at a time but they were a bit heavy for a boy so young. But, I showed him how to drag the slats over and help us put the bed together. I told him that is how you are helping put this bed together so that we can put the mattresses on it.

I complimented each of them for working on the project until it was done

Another time, during open house at school, the girls' teachers told us they wanted to move them into higher classes because they had such high scores on their AP tests.

My oldest daughter's open house had a display on the wall where there was a paper silhouette of three very large trees. On all these trees, the teacher had written words in place where you would normally see fruit. On the counter right below the silhouette trees they had paper silhouette cut outs which were paper cuttings with names of the parts of the paper that would match the names on the trees fruit.

My oldest daughter was asking if I would help her solve the riddle of how to match the pieces of paper with the words representing fruit to the correct tree paper silhouette.

Now, one tree was green as far as the canopy, one tree was red, one tree was orange. I was very surprised when I heard the teacher telling other parents that no one in her class was able to figure out how to place all the imaginary fruit that had the names written on them on the proper place of each tree.

I realized that this teacher had not been teaching the students basic concept on how to look up a word in the dictionary. To understand some of these words, I would need a dictionary to get the meaning. I was disappointed to see that this was a 4th grade teacher with these students.

So, what I did in explaining to my daughter is that this is nothing but a matching game. First of all, you have colors, so separate all the little imaginary fruits by color. She picked up a green one, look at the word, went to the green tree and look for the word that starts with a B because the word on the imaginary fruit is that of be careful. Now all you now all you're doing is matching the first letter then you're matching the second letter then you're matching, then the third letter. Next thing I know, my daughter matches all of them, putting all the imaginary fruit on the paper mache trees. The teacher was standing there in awe, the parents standing there with surprised looks on their faces.

The teacher came over to me and said, "I don't appreciate you teaching your daughter how to cheat."

"I said no ma'am, I didn't, but I taught my daughter how to look up a word in the dictionary. This is nothing but a matching game and that shows that you did not teach your students how to use a dictionary."

Another time, my youngest daughter and her 4th grade class were going to have a contest coming up. She said they would be giving presentations on a new idea they might have, an invention.

To make sure I understood what the class would be doing, I asked my daughter to repeat all of what was required and she was very clear.

Since she asked for my help, I began trying to figure out what I could help her with when it came to an idea for the project.

She told me that she would have to make a presentation about the project to her entire class.

There would be a contest to determine which presentation was the best. She wanted me to help come up with an idea, so we got to work on the presentation before we began on the project.

I asked her to focus on the homework it would take to make a great presentation.

One of the things I was very impressed with was that she learned that Mark Twain worked in the patent office, and he would interview children, asking their opinions and ideas.

Later, he wrote that between from 9 years old to 11 years old were demoralized by their parents.

The parents would tell them over and over that they did not deserve things, that they were not good enough, and would never achieve goals.

This negative thinking discouraged the children in this age group, limiting their paths in life and making them think they could not accomplish goals and dreams.

They would think that they weren't good enough to do things, didn't deserve rewards and did not see any reason to reach higher in life.

I thought this was very interesting because the way I taught my own kids was the total opposite, and that they could put together a plan to follow. This gave them a guideline through this path in life.

For the next couple of days, before the contest my daughter had entered, I am working with her on her presentation. During this time, I am pointing out to her how she is supposed to stand at attention while speaking, how her hands are supposed to be by her side most of the time, and how she is to look the judges straight in the eye with a smile at the same time.

She should try to get them to see the issue through their own eyes.

By doing this, the listeners would be thinking for themselves, but at the same time it would help her overcome stage fright and not be scared to make her presentation.

I told her she needed to look one inch above their eyes so she would not be afraid when she was making her presentation.

I would help her rehearse her presentation, and as the hours went by, I would point out small things to help her.

Finally, she was tired, I was tired, and since we felt like she could and would do a great job, she was ready.

When it was time for her to present her idea during the contest, she did a fantastic job.

She won the contest, accomplished her goal and, after a very impressive presentation, the judges made some very positive comments.

They couldn't believe that a fourth grade student could give a presentation equivalent to a first year college student.

All of this came from having a plan, putting the plan together, following the plan, and rehearsing the plan.

She was able to learn how to make the presentation, get input, do her research,

get a second opinion, and put one foot in front of the other. That led her down the path towards the goal of success.

As the children were getting older, but still young, people were already asking them what they wanted to be when they grew up.

What you plan to do once you graduate? They would ask.

What will you do when you get into the real workplace. Most of the time, most children say they don't know.

There is a good reason for the answer that they give, and that's because basically, they didn't get to view issues for comparison.

We were not in the workplace, so we have not had an opportunity to learn our interests, made mistakes yet because we haven't had the experience to understand.

I got a wild idea that every time we would go to a restaurant the kids would ask the waitress some questions, if she would let them.

One lady was very humorous, and had a fantastic personality. So, we would go to this one restaurant and always choose this waitress. One day, I talked to her and asked if she would come over to our table and talk about things she would change in her life if she could go back to her high school years.

What would she do differently than what she eventually did in life? The waitress looked at me with a surprise on her face. Her eyebrows went up, her eyes got very big and she had a kind of startled look on her face. I explained that we were not trying to get personal, but the reason I was asking was because my girls, before long, were going to be graduating from high school. And, I wanted them to be able to view other people's life experiences so that they can have a comparison as to what they're going to be facing in their real lives.

Actually, I decided we would call this a homeschool Science project and be asking survey questions.

I told her the girls didn't know about my idea yet, but when I got back over to the table, I would bring it up as soon as she come over to refill our glass of tea.

I explained that I was asking her permission to participate for the sake of my two girls. She looked at me with a tear in her eye and said something that really touched my heart.

"You know, it would have been nice if there were other parents like you, yes I'll be more than happy to do this for them," she said.

I went back to the table where everybody was sitting and told my girls that one day they were going to be graduating from high school. They were you're going to be looking at the real world and would always question what they were planning to do as far as a job, or a career. They would have to decide what kind of a goal they were going to set for themselves to live in the real world.

So what we're going to do starting now is when the waitress comes over, we're going to tell her that we are doing a Science project. We are asking survey questions about what she would do differently if she could go back in time down memory lane to her high school days. We will ask her if she will talk about it with us. Then, ask her if she would go back in time and tell us what she would do differently.

The waitress came over to our table and I told her the girls were working on a Science project, a survey, asking just a simple few questions, nothing personal.

They asked what she was thinking as a high school student about to go out into the real world.

Did you want to get married and have a family? Did you follow up on different careers that you might like to try? Or, would you have done something different?

The waitress began to tell her story. She told the girls that when she was in high school she had a sweetheart who had a nice job.

He wanted to get married have a large family. She thought that was great, so they graduated from high school, they got married and he had that great job.

Everything was going great and they had four children. She loved staying at home raising the children until one day her husband came home and said he was leaving and wanted a divorce. The waitress told us that she was in total shock because of all this time she did not have any type of career or college degree.

Other than being a homemaker, she had no other training. Now, since her husband left, and divorced her, she is raising the children alone, even though he now pays child support.

She is faced with being a waitress to support herself and her four children.

She said that if she could go back in time, had an opportunity to change something she would have had some type of career, some type of trade, maybe a college degree, so that if something like that did happen, she could always fall back on it and be independent.

She could be financially independent and raise her family.

Both of my girls looked at each other in awe because they couldn't believe what they had just heard.

I thanked the waitress very much for her time, and for taking part in this survey.

We finished eating and went home. I asked the girls what they thought about what the waitress had said. They talked about what the lady had said and how they learned from the message she had sent to them.

Here is a prime example of how you need to be careful with your words when talking to your kids. They can be very damaging instead of building high confidence.

Remember what Einstein said, most kids are demoralized by the age of 9 to 11 years of age because they're constantly hearing negative things.

My youngest daughter and I were going to the second stage of the contest she had won, and now was very good at giving her presentation. One day, I took her to a store grocery store. I stood right next to her while she would ask customers as they walked by if they would mind taking a part of a survey.

She said she was working on a Science project and wanted to get their opinions. It was very neat to see how customers would answer her questions. They would raise their eyebrows and kind of a smile and look at me and ask if this was my daughter.

Yes, she's my daughter, and they would say they were very impressed by her.

As the people came by and she would introduce herself to them, she would ask the questions and they were very cooperative in the survey. But, there's always one person, no matter where you're at, no matter where you work, when you're around a bunch of people there's always one that is negative.

There's always one who will throw a wrench in the gears, or there's always one who will try everything they can to shut you down.

It's called "misery loves company", and people do this sometimes unconsciously. They aren't aware of the fact that they do this and that the reason they did this is because of the intimidation or parental jealousy when they were at this very young age.

Their parents did not do anything with them like what my daughter and I were doing.

They didn't take the time to get involved with their children in a personal way, and therefore they are totally insulted by someone at a very young age who is getting to do something that they were not able to do or was not taught or given that special attention.

My daughter went over to a woman and introduced herself, explained what she was doing with the survey and asked if it would be all right to ask her a few questions.

The woman stood there with an appalled look on her face, her eyebrows came down, her face kind of turned cold her and her eyes turned very dark.

My daughter stood there with a smile waiting for the response of this individual. All of a sudden this woman started jumping down my daughter's throat calling her several different names.

When I stepped forward and was able to shut this down, my daughter began to cry. She asked why the woman was being so awful to her. "I haven't done anything, I'm just doing a Science project," she said.

I was trying to take care of my daughter, who was in tears.

I went over to the individual and talked to the woman and in a short period of time, she went over and apologized to my daughter.

The woman explained that her own father never did anything like this for her by helping become prepared for real life.

Someone had called the police because the woman had been screaming and my daughter was crying.

Once the woman explained what she had gone through to my child, the police took a report and left. That is what you call "misery loves company".

This next event that I did with my kids was something that a lot of people might have total different opinions about, some good, some OK, and there is always going to be somebody who would disagree with this.

When we were in high school, our parents always told us to be careful. "When you're with your friends, watch out, be aware of your surroundings. When you were with your friends at a party don't be drinking don't ride home with someone that's drunk," our parents constantly told us. "We don't want you to get hurt. We love you, we care about you, we're concerned about you," they would say.

My girls were getting older, and in a couple of years, and I was saying the same things to them. Kids respond the same ways we did back then. "I know, I know dad, I know dad, I'll be OK, dad.

I'll watch out as a dad, but for some reason there's something written by Mark Twain that says "experience is the best teacher". So, I decided to take my two girls, and my son, to the hospital.

"We're going to sit right next to the emergency doors are that means when the ambulance comes in and they take the patient out of the ambulance and rush them rush him to the emergency room, we're going to be sitting right here, close to this area so actually we are observers. I know my girls were kind of looking at each other like "dad why are we going to the hospital?" I explained to them that experience is the best teacher. " I've told you girls to be careful, and to be aware of your surroundings, but things happen when we least expect especially if we're not paying attention.

"So, logically, the reason we're going to sit here and wait for a patient to come in is so that you girls and your brother can see what it's all about. I don't want either of you to be on the stretcher coming out of an ambulance; so hopefully what you will see here will help you remind you to be careful."

We sat there for a while and then sure enough here came an ambulance rushing into the emergency area. The doors of the ambulance came flying open, the paramedics jumped out, and grab the handles of the cart where a patient is lying. We could see that the person was in extremely bad condition due to all the bloody soaked bandages that were all over him.

As they pulled the patient out of the ambulance, there was an IV bag on a holder. This IV bag fell off and was being drug on the ground. All of a sudden, my youngest daughter jumped up, ran over, picked up the IV bag as it was being drug on the ground, and walked alongside with the paramedics.

As they were wheeling the patient to the emergency room, all of a sudden the paramedics eyes grew as big as silver dollars, and their eyebrows raised up, and their mouths fell open. Their chins were about to hit the floor. I looked at them and told them there was nothing wrong with this little girl acting as an emergency first responder. I told them she was helping because the IV bag fell off the holder. I suggest all of us just keep going that direction, and the two paramedics looked at each other and just kind of smiled and looked at the little 11year-old little girl and nodded their heads as if to say thanks for the help. They rushed the patient down to the emergency room.

When we got there, a doctor stepped out and saw two paramedics, which is normal, but then saw this little girl with a big smile on her face holding the IV bag. Clearly, the doctor didn't know what to think. All of a sudden, his eyebrows started coming down, and his face started to tighten up a bit.

Because of what has happened in the past, I immediately leaned forward boldly hollered at the doctor.

Are we going to need another gurnery for another patient, I wondered. Or, is this little girl going to be wearing a coat just like the styles they are wearing today? The doctor looked at me and then turned to the paramedics and asked what had happened.

One paramedic told him and the doctor looked back at me ask is this your daughter?

"Yes, sir this is my daughter." He asked, "Would you mind if I pay her a compliment?" I replied, "Please, by all means. Would you pay her a compliment?"

The doctor's face turned into a smile. And his eyes sparkled. I could tell this man's response to a logical issue. The doctor walked over to my daughter and told her, "You know, I'm very proud of you assisting these two paramedics in an emergency situation, and if I could give an award, I would give you the award to the youngest person that I've ever had encountered who was an emergency first responder. I want to thank you so much for helping these paramedics. If you like helping people, maybe you might want to choose this as a career."

My daughter was just glowing like a beacon. "Yes Sir, thank you very much!" she said.

The doctor looked at me, and I at him, and I thanked him and told him to have a fantastic day.

As we went through the years of school, I was constantly taking the girls to meet other sales personnel and asking them to participate in this Science project, answering questions in a survey, until finally all the kids at some point in time in high school, would come up to me and say, "Dad, no more, no more, please dad! No more Science projects! We get it! We get it! We get the picture of what you're trying to tell us." I am OK with it now. My youngest daughter, who helped in that emergency with the first responder, graduated high school in three years, while taking college classes.

Now, at the age of 24 she has two college associate degrees, plus her certificate as a qualified Paramedic. She worked as a paramedic for two years, then wants to go on to become a doctor. However, she got married, has a family, and so there will be a delay in her education to achieving her goal.

During the time of her marriage, her husband earned his paramedics degree. Then he moved forward and earned his nursing degree.

He planned his future so that he would be making more money and be able to afford to help his wife, my daughter, go through a four year program to become a physician assistant. Everything was going great, my daughter was in her fourth year and preparing to graduate.

Then, one day, her husband, my son in law, told my daughter that he wanted a divorce.

He told her he was leaving her and their daughter, and taking everything, including their bank account.

Unfortunately, things happen in our lives that we least expect. This is what happened, and yes, this is what he did.

So, as parents, we stepped in for the moral, emotion support she needed in order to keep her dignity.

We helped our daughter with expenses so that she can complete her fourth year and graduate as a physician's assistant.

That positive and encouraging motivation from that doctor so many years before helped her a lot.

Finally the fourth year came to a close, and my youngest daughter was going to her graduation. The whole family attended, wanting to see the ceremony and give her a party after graduation. It was really nice, after all the pictures and all the gifts, and telling her how great she was, to tell her how proud we were of her accomplishments.

Even after the divorce, using courage, motivation, persistance and looking at things logically, she graduated!

Even though there were many emotional issues to deal with, she finished her schooling and graduated. It was really nice as everyone was preparing to leave as the party ended. She came over and shared a hug with me. As we hugged and embraced, I could hear and feel the tears that were being shed, as the sniffling continuing. I felt the love that was pouring out as she said, "Dad, thank you very much for being there with me, and thank you mom because I wouldn't have done it without you. I would not be where I am today if it wouldn't have been for the two of you being positive, encouraging, and motivation and helping me with my finances when my husband walked out and abandoned me and his daughter."

We both wiped up a lot of tears that day, something I will never forget.

Life is full of choices; Don't be afraid to ask someone for their opinion... It is all about choices

Eye to Eye

Why do you go to particular places on the spur of the moment? When you go somewhere, sometimes there are a lot of people. Have you noticed that you will find someone in the crowd and you make friendly eye-to-contact?

Why is it that sometimes you meet a person for the first time and feel an emotional connection, as if you already knew each other?

Why, after spending a few minutes talking to them, do you feel a warm, gentle secure, emotional bond? Why do you have the thought that you know them intimately?

For a couple of years, I have spent a lot of time sharing the "Science project" with strangers, and with my two young daughters and my very young son.

Now, the girls are entering high school and for some strange reason, I am getting the impression that I need to talk to them one more time, to find someone, a "stranger", who will participate in the Science project survey.

Both girls were involved in the project and will need to ask strangers if they would not mind participating in telling their life stories. I would like these people to talk about hte events and opportunities they had in high school and the decisions they made back then.

192

Now, if they go back in time, they can share whether or not they think they made the right decisions, or if those decisions were based on logic.

When they made that decision, would they keep it? Or, would they change it, and if so, why?

Like everyone else, I say my prayers, and in those prayers, I have asked where I could find the one person who needs to fulfill the promises of the Science project survey so they can validate that it works.

I want the validation so that I feel confident that both my girls will fully understand and get the point. I want them fully prepared to evaluate their choices before they make their final decisions. I want to know if they based those decisions on emotion or logic, because life is full of choices.

I look back at what happened one Friday. Before the day was over, I remember it was payday, and I had a strange thought: I needed to go to the mall. But, I began to think, I have visited a lot of malls, so which one should I go to?

I decided the one I shop at most frequently would be the one.

The next morning after breakfast, I told the children we should go to the mall and do a little shopping. The eyes of both my girls opened wide! Their smiles were even wider as they became excited.

All three said they would love to go and rushed to get ready for the shopping trip.

While on the way, the girls asked what we were going to buy. I suggested we look at some clothes, toys, and maybe something for their mother. They loved the plan.

When we arrived at the mall, we saw two different ways we could go. The girls asked which one we should take, the left or right. "Well, girls, trust your gut feeling," I told them. "My gut feeling is pulling me to the right; how do the two of you feel?"

I watched their faces as they looked to the left and then the right. "Dad, you have a good point, let's go to the right," both of them said.

As we walked along, one of the girls asked, "Dad, which store should we go in first?"

I responded, "If you see one we need to go into, just say so."

They saw one and wanted to go into it. So, we stopped, went inside and shopped, then went on to other stores.

After shopping in a few other stores, one of the girls asked if there was one in particular that I wanted to go into.

"Yes, there is," I said.

The girls told me they would go find it in the store directory, if I would tell them the name.

"It's just up ahead, around the corner," I replied. "I don't think it is in the directory."

I was using my gut feeling, and my gut feeling was that it was around the corner.

I noticed the odd looks on the faces of my girls. My son was very young, and was happy just to be at the mall.

The girls wanted to know what I was up to, what I had in mind, because they were a bit concerned.

With a smile, and waving my hands, I asked, "Why do you think I am up to something? Let's keep walking and shopping."

As we walked around the bend, I just stopped!

Again, the girls were concerned, "Dad, why did you just stop walking?"

I replied, "I am going to ask both of you girls to look ahead. Do you see anything out of the ordinary? Take your time and observe."

While watching their facial expressions, I noticed how their eyes became larger, their mouths opened, and their chins fell.

Both said, "Oh, my God!"

So, I asked them, "What do you see?"

"Dad, how is that possible?" was the response I got.

I asked what they saw, and one of them said, "Dad, it looks like the store has the brightest light inside the store! It makes the light rays shine out into the aisle of the mall where everyone walks!"

I asked the other daughter to describe it. "Dad, it looks like sun rays that shine through the window when the sun first comes up."

I responded, "You are good with your observations and descriptions. I agree with both of you. Now, what shall we do?"

"Dad, let's go check it out!" one of the girls said with excitement.

"I agree, let's go check it out," I said.

We continued to walk forward and stand in the very bright light that was coming from inside the store.

As we were standing in the doorway of the store, I saw that it was a store that sold women's clothing. We walked on in and a sales representative walked up to us and asked if she could help us.

As she was walking towards us, I notice that she had a glow around her. I noticed her eyes were sparkling as she walked up to us.

I complimented her on her wardrobe and told her that she looked very elegant.

"It really enhances your hairstyle, as well as the color of your eyes that sparkle," I said.

She thanked me and asked if she could be of help.

"Yes ma'am, if you don't mind, my two young girls and my little boy are with me. One day, they're going to be graduating from high school and they are going to be going out into the real world. We are working on a school Science project which entails asking a few minor questions, nothing personal, but would appreciate it if you would participate by just answering a few questions.

"It basically it means if you could go back in time to where you were in high school would you talk about the events that took place which was very important in the path you took after you graduated.

"Would you give your opinion about what you would do differently if you had the opportunity?"

She looked at me with a smile, then her face slowly dimmed. The sparkle in her eyes dimmed and she asked if these were my children. I said they were and she asked if the Science project was for them.

"Yes ma'am, this Science project is for them, and only them. It is a matter of comparison in learning because they want to learn."

She said she wished she had had a dad like me.

"If I would have, I would not be standing in this store selling clothes right now. I would be traveling and living a very nice, lavish life."

"Well ma'am, I appreciate your time, but if we can go back in time can you tell them what happened? And, what would you have done differently."

She smiled and looked at the girls in a very warm welcoming way.

She said she certainly would help by telling the story of when she was in high school. She had a sweetheart who was doing yard services for people. That was how he made his extra money, but then he got to the point where he could not handle doing all the yard work by himself. So, he got one of his friends to work for him.

In other words, he would have his friends go out and do the yard work and pay them, then keep the rest for himself. Basically, he had his own little business, which became very successful. At a very early age, he was already an employer and had employees.

He asked her to marry him, and she was happy and wanted to help him with his new company.

She could watch it grow and told him she would marry him.

When she told her parents about it, she was all excited. She wanted to marry him. However, her parents, who were from an average, blue collar family, living paycheck to paycheck, struggling to pay their bills, had known someone who had tried to start a small business, but failed. Therefore, her parents were constantly telling her that small businesses had a very high failure rate.

During this whole conversation, my oldest daughter watched, her eyes going from side to side. I watched her tilt her head to the left because that side of the brain is working the hardest; then I could see her head turned and tilt to the right, as the righthand side of the brain was starting to work.

I could tell that my oldest daughter was thinking about every word this woman said. Now the woman and I both noticed this, and then both girls' eyes were shifting in their heads tilting one way and or tilting the other way.

I asked the woman what she would have done differently, and what ended up happening.

She said well that she listened to her parents who were very concerned about her. But, they were very negative and not being open minded. The sad part was that they had not had good experiences being around people who wanted to step out and try to start a business.

"They could have been far more positive, encouraging me," she said. "As an end result, I did not marry my high school sweetheart. As of today, he is very successful, has a very big business and does all the things we talked about doing, like traveling.

"He married my best friend, and of course, we are all friends and we stay in touch with one another."

As this meeting was coming to a close, the woman asked me if she could share a hug with each of the kids.

I said, "Yes, ma'am that would be fine." And she did.

I noticed that she whispered something in the ear of my oldest daughter from watching her facial expression. Then, she asked if we could share a hug, and I agreed.

I told her I really appreciated her taking part in participating in this survey.

"I could tell you the end results of the survey but we'll just leave that chapter in a book remaining a mystery until it happens, but the meantime, thank you, God bless you, and you have a fantastic day," I said.

She had a tear in her eye as we said goodbye. "Little girls, you got a heck of a dad, so pay attention and don't get frustrated with all the things that he's trying to do to help you," she said.

On our way home, I asked the girls what they thought about the woman's story and about the opportunity that she had when she was in high school. And, then unfortunately, because of the negative unsupportive parents, due to the lack of knowledge and experience, they knocked this woman's goal out of existence. Both girls voiced their opinions, but my oldest daughter said that it could happen to anybody.

"If I was to try to do this, would you support me?" she asked.

I said absolutely I would because I have a tremendous amount of knowledge and background that would help you put a plan together, and to just let me know if that happens and we would work on it.

On The Job Experience

One day, the girls asked me about the day I took them to the hospital. They saw the patient coming out of the ambulance, and then they saw the patient rushed to the emergency room.

Their question was: "Why did you take us there?"

I began to tell them they had to see firsthand what would happen to you when you think you're invincible.

"You might think this would never happen to you. Or, something like this will never happen to you at any given point in time in your life, but because you saw reality based on logical common sense, you realize that you are not invincible and that this can happen to you.

"These things do happen, especially if you don't pay attention to your surroundings in your everyday life.

"I would like for you all to keep in mind that every night when you say your prayers, you ask God for guidance, protection, and assistance, so that your life will be a safe road which you travel now.

"For example, if you use your imagination, your creative thinking, there are times when you are going to be at the wrong place at the wrong time, which could be devastating. Now, the good Lord answers your prayers and he is everywhere you ask him to be, especially when you need him. For example, if he were to tell you in a foreign language that you were going to be at the wrong place at the wrong time. What would you do?

"Most likely you would ignore the situation, because you do not understand the message that the good Lord is trying to give you.

198

For example, maybe you were about to possibly be in a car wreck, then all of a sudden you saw this flash before your eyes of the patient that was on the gurney in the hospital, all bandaged up, bloody, what would you think at that point in time?"

The kids all made the comment that they would clearly understand that the good Lord would be trying to get their attention, and tell them that there's a bad issue ahead. He would be saying the road that they're traveling has something wrong, and they needed to be careful. I thanked them and told them I was very proud of each of them. I was happy that they all came up with the same conclusion. I told them that they would never know if a year from now, or five years, or maybe ten years down the road, they might see something pop up in their vision warning them of danger.

"You better pay very close attention and react in a very cautious, logical manner, so that you will not be at the wrong place at the wrong time. I don't want to come up to the hospital knowing that you've been admitted because of a bad accident, which could be fatal. I don't want to have to go through that," I said.

As the years have passed, each child has come up to me and thanked me with emotion, eyes filled with tears, and hugging me, wanting to tell me a story. I reminded them to pay attention to their surroundings at all times.

My youngest daughter, while driving, was traveling in a lot of snow on the highway. As she was coming up to an overpass, she saw a lot of cars going slow, some going fast, but before they could get to the overpass, all of a sudden, an image of the hospital incident flashed in front of her eyes.

Using logic and common sense, she pulled over and got totally off the freeway.

The person riding with her asked if something was wrong and if she was all right.

My daughter told me that when she noticed cars starting to slow down, she watched the taillights as they were reaching the peak of the overpass.

Then, she saw smoke and saw some cars stopping at the top of the overpass.

She was unable to see what had happened on the other side, but found out that there had been a car accident which caused several cars to pile up, and there were several injuries, and some casualties.

My daughter just simply looked up at the sky and said, "Thank you Lord, thank you Lord, thank you Lord!"

Self Control

Another day, my oldest daughter was traveling on the freeway when she came up to the exit off the freeway and drove up to the light, which was red. She sat there waiting for the light to turn green, when all of a sudden, the hospital incident flashes before her eyes.

She didn't move, thinking cautiously, and looked back and forth at oncoming traffic.

The cars behind her were honking their horns for her to go on through the intersection. She hesitated to move forward when all of a sudden, a full size 4 X 4 truck ran the red light, through the intersection and would have clearly T-boned her small sedan.

How many injuries and casualties do you think would have been caused if she had not waited? She pulled over to the side of the road, extremely shook up.

The emotional aftermath was trying to surface, and hit her like a ton of bricks.

As the car came to a complete stop, her knuckles had turned white due to holding on to the steering wheel so tightly. Her eyes began to flood with tears, as she was trying so hard, logicall, not to make any screaming sounds in front of her daughter and son. But, the emotion took over.

All of a sudden, she just started trying her hardest to muffle her screams as the tears flowed down both sides of her face.

Then, the kids asked. "Mom, are you OK?" with great emotional concern as their eyes were filling up with tears.

She bolted out of her seat, shoved the car door open, and it came close to breaking at the hinge.

She bolted to the passenger door, opened it, grabbed both of her kids, pulled them out of the car, all while tears poured from her eyes.

She was confident now, they were safe. But, all of a sudden, the emotional ton of bricks hit. She stood there, embracing her kids in her arms. The tears just flooded her eyes, running down her face. She did not hold back! Finally, she gave a grateful, happy meaningful scream at the top of her lungs. To think that all three of them would have been killed! With faith in spirit, mind and heart, she knew God had watched over them, protected them and brought them to safety.

She looked up and said, "Thank you my Lord! Thank you, my Lord, my God!"

Think about this. Has anything similar happened to you?

My son told me of a situation where he was on the freeway when he saw a very dark rain cloud. Knowing that he was about to drive into a heavy rainstorm, he drove on, but suddenly the rain started coming down so hard that visibility was at a minimum.

He told me he could hardly see the taillights in the car in front of him.

Then, all of a sudden, the same flash that he had seen at the hospital emergency entrance when he was a child flashed before his eyes.

He then realized that something up ahead was very bad.

So, he cautiously he got totally off the freeway and sat waiting for the rain to let up.

Suddenly, he heard loud thunder. Of course, he was kind of curious because he had not seen any lightning.

He thought that it was kind of odd sounding thunder. Actually, he discovered, what he was hearing was the sound of automobiles crashing into each other as a car pileup began.

For some reason, someone had caused a fender bender, which caused a pileup.

As the rain started slacking off, his view of the scene became very clear and he could see all the vehicles all piled up, smashed into each other. As he sat in his vehicle on the side of the road, he just looked up to the sky and said, "Thank you Lord, thank you Lord, Thank you Lord!"

Advice from the Past

My oldest daughter was in her senior year of high school and soon to graduate.

She was working part time at a clothing store and one day came home with a very concerned look on her face. I saw a little fear, so we sat at the table and she asked me if I would spend some time with her talking about the subject of starting her own business, being her own boss, and working from home.

With my eyebrows raised, I was thinking, "Oh, my gosh, what has she come into contact with now?"

But I gave her every opportunity to talk to me, and I never said anything negative to cut her down, or tell her this was a bad idea.

Because, first of all, there are little things called "details" which are very important. It can change a viewpoint and change thinking and help make a final decision about an issue.

So, I said "OK" with a smile, "I'm listening, what are your questions?"

With a very serious look on her face, she told me how the woman in the clothing store, years ago, made a comment to her.

When I asked what the woman said, she said, "If an opportunity ever comes up, jump on it and don't let anything get in front of you."

I looked at her with a smile.

"So, there's a possibility that this very same type situation has presented itself at my job."

Whoa! As I looked at her with a big smile, I told her to tell me what was going on.

At first, she was hesitant, so I asked her if she had a plan. She said she did, and that her plan was to learn anything and everything that she needed to learn to keep from making mistakes that other people have made. She said she wanted to have a better chance of becoming successful her first time in business. She said she wanted to go in as partners with her husband, some day.

I told her I was very impressed.

"Go get a new spiral notebook and a pen and we're going to sit down and you're going to write notes in this notebook and you're going to use it as a manual, or a starter kit, because you can't rely on your memory for everything that we're going to talk about.

"The first thing is why small businesses generally fail."

She asked why we would talk that instead about people who are successful.

"You have a good point, but I would like to point out that if you learn from all other mistakes people make, then most likely you're not going to make the same mistakes," I explained.

"Those mistakes caused other people to have to close their business. Now, let's look at the first part. If you're going to start a small business, your partner has to be a business partner, even though the two of you might be in love or you might be thinking about hormones. You have to remember that your partner has to be on the same page, same paragraph, same line that you are on, so that the two of you work together as a fantastic team.

"Do you have any questions about what I've said so far?"

"No dad", she said. "I have no questions."

"OK," I went on, "Let's talk about the business that failed. First of all, you need a very charming personality. For example, you know why we always go back to the same waitress every time when we go to the restaurant that we eat at?

"The reason is because we like her charming personality as well as her service. A lot of times when people start up a small business they forget to look at their competition. They forget to look for a good location, and then it comes to the partners and whether or not they see eye to eye, to avoid conflict.

"Now will you tell me about what is going on as far as this business that you're talking about and seem to be quite excited about?"

My daughter began to tell me that in this day and time of the computer age, there is a very large demand for people to build websites for people who are starting their businesses.

I was impressed that she had done her homework.

"Now tell me what is going on with your plans right now so that I can be more help to you. It is important that you also see things that are down this path that you wanting to travel.

"Yes Sir, dad, at my job where I work, one of my coworkers has a boyfriend that comes in and visits with us when we're getting close to closing time."

"OK, and what is exactly going on?" I asked.

"The boyfriend is always telling the coworker and myself that he works for a small company that builds websites for a small businesses, trying to get started in the business of advertising.

"He is constantly telling us that he could run the business all by himself. He is self-confident that he could be very successful while his boss is in a very sunny location, sipping on some refreshments, while enjoying an oil rub down, at the same time.

"The boyfriend is certain and confident he can do this because he has done it multiple times. He has run a business while his main boss is away on business."

So I asked my daughter if she saw this as a window of opportunity that had walked in and was standing right in front of her.

"Yes, Sir, dad, that's what I am seeing. However, there is one problem that I don't like. I don't want to disrupt my coworker's good relationship with her boyfriend."

I asked my daughter if her co-worker seem to be positive, encouraging and motivating to her boyfriend to put one foot in front of the other and actually start putting together his self-owned and directed business by himself.

"No dad, she doesn't seem to be very positive and encouraging about what he wants to do. She's constantly asking him questions in the form of fear thinking emotionally to whether or not he can actually do the business that he's talking about.

"So, dad I am asking you, what would you suggest I do in this situation?"

My question to her was, "Well, what do you want to do? You want this business? Do you want to accomplish this goal that you've heard from someone else who had a fabulous opportunity right in front of her and turned it down and will spend the rest of her life regretting it?

"Now, are you going to think about this emotionally, are you gonna think about it logically, or do you want to take a chance and make a go of it?"

"Yes Sir, dad, logically I want to do this and I feel very confident that everything you've told me about is in line for the two of us to become successful in running our own business.

"But, I don't want to take away my co-worker's boyfriend," she added.

"Well, sweetheart, just be yourself. Logically you are very positive and courageous in motivation. You have a fantastic, humorous personality, plus you have a tremendous amount of knowledge as to why small businesses fail, therefore you are a very educated, knowledgeable young woman that any guy would need to have as a business partner," I said.

"There is no need for you to wear fake eyelashes, blinking your eyes a lot, wearing extremely snug pants, and displaying body language you don't need to use. You don't need any of that. I would tell that guy that you believe he can do this, that it can be done, and you will help him get there, and if he wants you to help him, just give you a call. Then, don't be surprised if he asks you to go out on a date. Because if it was me, and I was in his shoes, and I wanted to start a business, I would be scared, but I would also know that I had just met someone who is very knowledgeable, very positive, very encouraging and very motivated.

"I would see that you are making a choice between dating someone like that, versus dating someone who is scared and thinking with emotion who doesn't have knowledge.

"Which one of these two young women would I be asking out on a date? I know it is very important to have a very educated motivated supportive business partner who thinks with logic while making a business successful.

"Now, let me point out something that needs to be very important to you. I have a great deal of admiration for what women actually do.

"It's the workload that women take on that should be appreciated, but a lot of times are not. You are going to have to take on the role of a girlfriend, a CEO, a vice president, a foreman, and later, a mother. You're going to have to stay on top of this guy and let him know that the two of you need to get to work and be successful because you have got bills to pay. And, you need to do it with kindness and love, and a sense of humor."

The next thing I know, my daughter is bringing her new boyfriend over to the house for me to meet. We sat down and discussed the plans that they put together. I must compliment my daughter on doing a very good job of putting a plan together.

They got married and shortly after their marriage they gathered all the equipment they needed for the business, and the son-in-law slowly gained clients while working and building websites.

My daughter was still working at the clothing store until they were able to financially break free and start their own business.

At the age of 21, she and her husband decided that their business was doing really well and decide they were moving to another city in another state.

My son in law thanked me many times for showing my daughter how they could work together to succeed.

Before they moved, they came over and visited to say goodbye. At first, it was all great fun, laughter, talking about the success they had in the past, and their goals for the future.

Finally, it was time for them to leave, that time that no one likes when a loved one is involved in a farewell.

I saw tears in my son-in-law's eyes as he shook my hand and thanked me for all I had done for them.

"Thank you so much for what you taught your daughter and myself," he said.

I gave him a big hug that added more tears to his eyes. He told me that his father never did anything like that for him.

When it was time to say goodbye to my daughter, we stood, each with our arms open and hugged. We both tried to hold back the tears, but ended up sniffling. I could feel her body shaking as she said, "Thank you dad, thank you. I never would have never made it if it weren't for you and mom I love you dad. Thank you so much!"

They got into their car, waved and drove down the road and faded in the distance.

A Goal-Some Would Say Out of Reach

My son wanted to get into the high school band and play an instrument.

The issue was that he's never played a musical instrument and did not know how to read music. But, he was determined to achieve first chair, but with his exciting using his imagination he wants to accomplish first chair, the top player with an instrument, a trumpet.

I asked him if he had a plan, and he asked if I would help him set one up.

I saw the sparkling in his eyes and glow in his face. I told him there were a lot of things to do to cover all the details so he could reach his goal.

"First of all, we're going to sit down and we're going to talk about the physical characteristics of a trumpet. Then, we're going to go through and learn all different mechanics of the trumpet then we're going to go through and learn where the most power comes from when you're blowing this instrument.

"Then we're going to ask your mother to teach you how to read music and learn tempo. One thing that is most important is that you have to have the willpower and want to learn everything. Proficiency. There are going to be times when you're going to have to be tough. There will be times when the music is not going to sound right.

"But, since we have taken this whole 'reaching your goal' plan and put it into different sections, you must perfect each section by the time you pull everything together to accomplish your goal".

He looked at me and said he would do that, if I would help him learn to complete these different tasks. I agreed, saying I would help, but he had to do it on his own. I told him he would have to practice, learn the music, practice and continually repeat the process.

"You have to put one foot in front of the other to try to make it, and we're going to try to perfect every detail separately, I told him.

By doing this in this manner, he was able to win the award of the first chair in band in the first nine weeks of school!

But, he lost first chair, and was in last chair because he became over confident. He wanted it back, and said he would regain his first chair by the end of the school year, and he did.

Progress of Self Confidence

While still in high school, he joined JROTC. Then one day, he came upto me and his mother and said he wanted to go into the military. Parents are very proud of their children who want to go into the military, but they also have to deal with a parent's worst nightmare, that their son or daughter may one day not come home walking on their own two feet but would be carried in a box with a flag draped over it.

I asked my son why he wanted to join the military.

"Dad, whether you realize it or not you raised me as though you were a military Drill Sergeant. That's why I feel I need to go into the military."

When he said that, I did not know what to think. I did not know what to say. I just wondered, what in the world I had done. I was very proud of him for wanting to go into the military, but I feared a parent's worst nightmare as he went to enlist. I was there with him making sure that he fully understood everything that was going on, and that everything has to be in the contract he was about to sign.

He was thinking about different paths in the military and I pointed out that he needed to work on making a very high score on his test. I told him then he would have more options to pick from when it came to his job.

I reminded him of the time we went to play paintball and there was a guy dressed up like a sniper.

My son was all "gung ho" because he was wearing Army fatigues and wanted to go with the boy who was dressed in a military uniform, the sniper. We parted ways, with me telling him that we'd meet back at the truck later. I told him to have fun, be careful and make his shots count.

Later, when he came back to the truck, he was very tired, his feet were dragging, and he seems to be all shot up with paintballs. I looked at him and started to ask what happened.

But, all of a sudden, he said he didn't want to talk about it. So, we left, and went to sit in the air conditioning and eat lunch.

I asked him if he knew what had happened, and I was trying not to laugh.

He was getting mad because he thought I was laughing at him, and joking around.

I told him I was not laughing at him, but was thinking about this really hilarious thing I saw on a comedy show.

But, I suggested that, sooner or later, if he didn't mind, maybe he could tell me what happened. He slowly went from a very angry looking emotional expression on his face to laughing and said, "Dad, I cannot believe I was so stupid!"

I asked what had happened, because I really wanted to know. I was trying to keep from laughing when he started telling his story.

"That sniper to told me to walk out to the end and fire my paint guns so he could find out where everybody was at so he could shoot them. I said OK. I can't believe I was so stupid! I walked out there and got all shot up with paintballs!"

I asked if the sniper had shot all the people who were shooting at him, and he said the guy just disappeared.

"He didn't cover my back at all!"

I told him that I hoped this incident would help him think more logically in the future.

"Thank you, dad," he laughed. "You have the darndest ways of getting my attention; for me to learn things. I just want to say, 'thank you', Dad. I love you, and I know we've just talking in this restaurant, but I want to give you a hug."

So, we both get up out of our chairs, we embrace each other, and he said, "Thank you, dad, I love you."

I told him I loved him and was proud of him, my son.

He enlisted in the military as a Marine to become an aviation mechanic.

Most parents, I would think, dread the day when they take their child to the airport to be flown to boot camp in full uniform.

While we were standing in line waiting for him to board the airplane, there were a lot of people standing in line waiting to be called to be seated.

Finally, the plane come in, passengers disembark, and as the airplane was being refueled, and restocked, the lady at the end of the tunnel started calling to start boarding. We were standing probably about 20 feet away when my son's number was called.

His mother walked with him up towards the personnel that collects the tickets, and I stood while his mom got to exchange hugs and kisses and many tears with her son, knowing that he is going to boot camp.

My son looked up at me, and I was looking at him.

By the expression on his face, I could tell he wanted to give me a hug, but mom was still hugging and kissing on him and the lady who collects the tickets was constantly saying he needed to get aboard.

I could see his red face and the tear in his eyes as he was saying goodbye to his mother.

I felt like he was saying that he was sorry he did not get a chance to share a hug with me to say goodbye.

This is an act of love moment that I will never forget. I was remembering when my son told me I was like a drill sergeant, and all of a sudden, I pushed my cap forward, put my hands behind my back, stomped one foot next to the other and hollered, maybe louder than the intercom. "Private First Class James Markham, you need to take control of the situation and walk back here and give your dad a hug!"

My son looked around and you could see his face light up as he told his mom to excuse him for a minute.

He turned to the lady collecting the tickets and said they had time for a minute, and walked back to me.

"Dad why did you have to do that," he asked. "Because, son, this is what you call a "moment of closure.""

We embraced each other and shared a hug as we both began to sniffle.

We were both trying to hold back the tears and I said, "I know, I know."

The tears fell on my shoulders and went through my shirt and soaked onto my skin as I told him that I loved him.

"I'm proud of you, son. Do your best. As he sniffled and thanked me, he said, "I love you, dad. I'll do my best, dad.

As he's walking towards the lady to hand her his ticket, I hollered one more time, "Soldier, this is a war; this is a war between emotion and logic. You have to get rid of all of your emotion and go through this boot camp with pure logic and you will win the war. Proud of you son, love you, son. Give it your best shot!"

He handed his ticket to the lady, gave his mother one last hug and kiss, and he walked through the tunnel and faded towards the airplane.

I looked at my wife and she had a look of embarrassment and humiliation on her face. Her eyes were dark, and she asked, "Why, in front of God and everybody else, did you have to do that?"

I turned and looked at all the people standing in the line waiting to board the airplane, and saw a lot of men with moisture in their eyes. I asked them if there was a problem and several of them said the same thing, one man said, "My dad never did anything like that for me in all my years. I must compliment you as a father. I wish you could have been my father when I was your son's age."

I thanked them all very much and said that this story of parent's and their children's lives can intensify the love and bond them with respect to the utmost degree. I told them this was one of the most important things they could ever share with their families.

You, my readers, need to love your children, simply spend time with them, one on one, and as a family group. Do all three exercises so that you and each of your children, and your family, will progress together and you will enjoy the prosperity, harmony, and the experience of bonding that is so strong that nothing could actually break this bond.

So far, I have found nothing that can break it. Constantly give your kids a hug, no matter how old they are, or how tall they are, and you always want to tell them you love them, and that you're proud of them.

Now you've read the book!

*   Go back and study, master the exercises.
*   Use logic versus emotion quotes to expand your creative thinking.
*   Exercise and use definitions of traits to develop their character.

From there, you can help anyone and everyone you want to help: spouse, children, relatives, and coworkers.

*   You will help people see a bright light and path towards their accomplishing their goals.
*   You will help them see through their own eyes how to establish a well-organized plan so they can compare their options before they make a good logical decision.

The Adventures of Character That Shaped America

This timeline of the Americans Old West is what won the West:

A chronically ordered list of events that took place to help shape the region are countless. They were made by people of outstanding character. That is what has shaped what happened in the past, as well as the future of this country, The United States of America.

The character of a person consists of all the qualities they have. They make them their plan from a form of other people or places. Perhaps there is a positive or negative emotional versus logical side to his or her character that you have not seen yet, or, he or she has not seen yet.

We never really see what we are learning with or the emotional residue of engaging in the mildest of negative talking to ourselves.

We often don't realize how negative thoughts impact our mood and behavior at any given moment. As a result, we end up doing or not doing things our rational mind wants us to do.

If you're thinking and speaking emotion, you will talk about how unfair life is; you'll start to act according to that review, perceiving slights when none exist, or as studies have shown, putting less effort into your work because you've already determined it is not worth accomplishing anything.

This unfair view will quickly become your reality.

On the other hand, think and speak logical results in good common sense. The person who receives success as if it were just around the corner will not only work their tails off to achieve it, but be in energized and alive to it and all the while acting on the fundamentals view of success.

To be clear, believing you will be successful is only one part of success.

Now, I want to ask some questions: What is your definition of character? How do you see it? How do you think it affects your life? Does it have a major or minor impact on others? Does your character have any positive or negative effects towards your wanting to accomplish promotions or goals you so desire to achieve?

Think about this: You are invited to a party. There are a lot of people, some you know. At the party is a very the variety of drinks and food. As the party goes on, there are some people acting humorous. When you are well relaxed, you are just being yourself, even acting a little silly. What you do not know is that someone is videotaping the party. As the party came to a close, the host tells you goodnight, saying he hopes you enjoyed the party. You assure him that you had a wonderful time.

He stops you and adds that next week he wants to invite you back over to watch some home movies. You agree and say you are looking forward to it.

The following Saturday, you show up at the friend's apartment and the host opens the door. You exchange greetings and sit down and he offers you a drink. You notice the host has a beer in his hand so you decide a beer would be fine.

The evening gets underway, when the host says he wants to show some home movies.

"I need your opinion as to which one would be the best to enter into the world's funniest home video contest," he says.

"Hopefully, I might stand a chance at winning the $10,000 first prize. I would just be ecstatic if that happens.

"So, I would like to ask for your opinion as we watch these movies. See which one you think would be the one I should enter into the contest that has the best chance of winning." So, as the movies begin, everyone wants another beer.

"Sure, there are plenty in the icebox," your host says, "help yourself." You go get yourself a fresh beer thinking to yourself that it would to have some popcorn to go with the beer.

You ask what type of events the host video taped.

"I'm glad you asked, because this movie I just recently recorded, or this is the one I taped a year ago might be the best. Let's watch it and you tell me if I should enter it.

He pushed the play button as the movie starts. You see some of the people looking like stiffs at an event, and you also notice some people in the movie as if they had plenty of alcohol to drink.

You find this very humorous; you know that what the people are doing is pretty funny.

You continue to watch the movie and notice that there is a person whose face you cannot see.

You do notice that person in the movie is acting like an overrated clown.

This person is acting like an idiot! What a fool!

As you are watching this person you do not notice that you are constantly criticizing this person and their actions.

All of a sudden you get very silent. Your eyebrows shoot up, your eyes grow as large as silver dollars, your mouth falls open, your chin falls in your lap and then you realize what is going on.

The person in the movie turns around and you now recognize the person you were criticizing is You!

Making life decisions and changes

There was a company where I was employed as a supervisor in a fab department overseeing welders and fitters. This company hired many people from other countries: China, Pakistan, Muslims, El Salvador, plus EUS citizens, black Americans, Mexicans, Latinos, and whites.

Now all of these people were basically blue-collar workers.

One day, one of my crewmembers asked me if I could help him with an issue. I asked him what the issue was.

The welder, an African American, with a very cocky attitude was trying to have a very highly sophisticated attitude. He told me that he was taking a night class at a college to achieve his degree in drafting. The problem was that the teacher, or professor was not covering all of the material that was needed to pass the exams. I asked if he had a book that he can use for a reference.

He told me that when the instructor tells the students that they will be taking a lot of notes, questions from those notes will be on the exam.

"When the instructor is reading out of his book, for example, he gives information out of chapters one through four. When it is time for us to take the exam, we study our notes very thoroughly for the exam."

The guy told me that when the students take the exam, there are questions on the exam that are not in their notes.

He said they all take the exam and get it handed back with a very low score, and they have failed the exam.

There is more than one way to resolve this problem, I told my co-worker. One, get a book to use as a reference to read a chapter ahead. Everyone has a boss, I told him. The issue here is the teacher.

It turns out the teacher was taking information from chapter five, one that they haven't even reviewed in class.

He was putting questions in the exam where there was no way the students could get the answers all correct to pass the exam.

The welding student was suspicious, but not sure how to approach the problem. He asked for my help, asked what he needed to do to pass the course.

He asked if I went to college and I told him I had gone and earned a four-year degree in the science of welding.

He asked if I had any of the problems which he had described.

I told him that I did have similar issues, but I was able to get them corrected. Again, he asked if I would help with his issue.

I needed more information, so I needed to ask more questions. He said he had already described the problem.

I saw that the man was thinking and speaking very emotionally due to his failing his college exams.

But, regarding the issue at hand, he was searching for a logical answer to resolve the problem. The college semester would one day end, and he was very scared he was not going to pass the course, nor get his degree Along with that, he would be out of a lot of money he had spent on the course.

He was in a hurry to find a solution and that is why he had asked for help to solve the problem. But, he didn't want to hear my advice. Everyone knows what happens when they do something in a hurry; most of the time they make mistakes. By the time they fix their mistakes, they realize they should have taken a little more time. They think to themselves, "I could have done this the right way the first time, then not have to go back to fix the mistakes I made."

Let me ask you some of the questions I asked the welding student, which he answered.

Me: Are you coachable?

Him: Yes, Mr. Markham, I am.

Me: Are you open-minded?

Him: Yes, Mr. Markham, I am.

Me: Are you willing to learn something new?

Him: Yes, I am.

I told him that his answers were great. Then, I told him, I wanted to point out that if he thinks is so sophisticated that he laughs or mock my way of helping him, then we needed to stop right there. "This is not second grade. This is a method and if you act foolish, I will not help you again." He laughed and snickered then said he would agree to work with me.

About a third of the tutoring time, he showed what he thought was sophistication. He said that this material was bogus, and he did not like my method.

I told him that since he felt that way, the class was terminated. I noticed that his eyes widened, his smile melted away, and his mouth fell open. His chin hit the floor.

I told him, that he needed to get his job (at work) done. "This is in your booth. You need to get this job done, because that is your job as a welder," I said. Then, I walked away. The welder in the booth next to the guy I was trying to help overheard the conversation.

One week later, that guy, a Mexican American Latino asked me if I would help him with an issue. I just looked at him, but he said he would do anything I asked him to do. "If you tell me to do jumping jacks, I will do them, no questions asked.," he promised.

The look on his face was so sincere that I stood looking at him and thought to myself, "This man seems to be very serious."

I smiled and raised my eyebrows, said, "OK, do 25 jumping jacks."

With no surprise on his face, and no hesitation, he did the 25 jumping jacks. After he finished, with a happy smile on his face, he said he was ready. I asked him the same questions I had asked the other welder. This second welder said he would do whatever I told him to do, and called me "Sir".

Now this young man was very thin and covered from head to toe with tattoos, with very large donuts holes in each earlobe. He was very shy, and when there was any trouble or controversy coming his way, he would hide or vanish, to avoid any type of confrontation.

We started the course, a method which is new to everyone. When we finished, he said he had "gone from a mouse that would hide from everyone if there was a problem.

He soon became an admired, respected leader and spokesman for all the Mexican Americans in our fabrication department. Every day, he would come up to me with a handshake and brotherly hug, thanking me, addressing me as "Boss Man".

I asked him to tell me in layman's terms what I did for him. He said the best way he could describe it was like this: Because of self-doubt and insecurity due to thinking emotionally, I had pointed out the difference of consequences between that and learning the value and rewards and beliefs of thinking and speaking logical common sense.

He explained how he had felt. "I felt like I had a metal band around my head. This band felt like it was blocking me from everything that I wanted to achieve in life. Now, this metal band had a bunch of locks on it like a chain link, but as you were teaching me your techniques, your method, the locks started opening and falling off, one at a time until there were no more locks. Then, the metal band of emotional uncertainty and self-doubt just disappeared. My wife says I am an entirely different person. She is very impressed."

The African American welder I had started to teach, but told I would not help, came to me and apologized for his actions. Then, he asked if I would pick up and continue to teach him my technique or method. I would observe his facial expressions, then say I would think about it.

This went on for a couple of months, while I was teaching other coworkers. Now, the first welder was getting close to graduation, but he still was faced with the same problem. The instructor was not teaching the material that was needed to pass the major exam.

One day, the welder asked me again to help him. The look on his face was pitiful.

He said "I have spent all this money for this course, spent all this time going to night school, I will end up with nothing but a triple loss if I give up."

With the long face and sad eyes, he added, "I thought I was someone. I thought I knew everything to where I did not need to learn something new." With moisture in his eyes, he begged me "Will you please continue to teach me?"

I again told him to let me think about it and turned around and walked away. The welder just emotionally cratered. Then, I turned around faced him and said, "I have given this a lot of thought. Now, do you really want to pick up where we left off?"

His face glowed like a beacon, his eyes sparkled with a smile a mile wide. He hollered, "Yes, Sir!"

So by learning to think and speak logically, understanding the rule of rewards, plus the benefits, we finished the course. He discussed the matter with the Dean of the college and during the conversation, the welder was able to present himself with a very diplomatic character. "Is this something we can take care of, Sir?" he asked the Dean.

The class was furnished with a substitute teacher who finished teaching the materials the students needed to pass the exam.

Every student passed and got their degrees.

One person thinking and speaking emotion as he or she learns to think and speak logic alters their character, then they can enjoy the rewards of success.

All of these people that I helped had a different promotion goals that they were trying to achieve. As I worked with each one, I would ask them what their goal was? Did they have a plan? They would stand with an empty look on their faces. Then, with the slightest of an outburst, they would start talking about why they felt they have not received the promotion they wanted to achieve.

It is very interesting that all of these people had one thing in common: they would gripe, complain, and whine and come up with multiple excuses, based on their attitudes. For example, their race, gender, skin color, culture, and religion, their faith, their feeling of not being accepted or respected as human beings.

How does this affect their character? Ask yourself if you were the person interviewing them for a job where they would have to deal with the public.

What would be your decision regarding hiring them? Based on their continuous whining and complaining about their surroundings of society, the chances are you would not hire them.

Now, let me tell you about The "tool room man".

This person was very young married with a young daughter. Making barely enough money to pay bills. This is where both spouses need to work in order to enjoy living a good life. This African American walked around with a fictitious limp, and his pants would be down half off his backside, and his shirttail flying in the breeze. He wore a cap on sideways with the "rake" stuck in his hair.

As I would pass his area, I would noticed that he was always reading a book. So, I asked him if he liked reading? "Yes Sir, I love to read books and soak up all the information I can," he said.

I found it very interesting to see someone who has such a low paying job want to climb the ladder and become very successful, and accomplishing a goal through knowledge. One day, while passing the tool room, I saw him standing outside the door. I noticed what looked like a scared look on his face. He looks at me and said, "Sir, may I talk to you for just a moment?"

Well, of course, I said yes and asked what he wanted to talk about.

I could tell he was very nervous because of the quivering in his voice. "Sir, Mr. Markham, I have a goal I would like to achieve. I am asking you if you will help me achieve it, Sir," he said.

With a smile on my face and my eyebrows raised, I asked what he wanted to achieve. The look on his face was surprising.

"Mr. M., you addressed me as Sir. For that, I thank you. And, I do not understand why you address me as Sir."

"Well, that's because I look at everyone as equal. I will give you 100 percent respect as long as I get 100 percent respect in return," I explained.

I noticed him taking a large swallow and so I asked if he was all right with that. The look on his face of pride and enjoyment said what I wanted to know.

"Yes, Sir, Mr. Markham," he said.

"Now, what do you want to talk about?" I asked.

"There is a job offering coming up and I want to achieve the position, Sir."

"What is the position? Do you have a plan?" I asked him.

"Yes, Sir, the position is to become an assistant manager at a fast food restaurant. My plan is to ask if you will teach me a plan in which I can accomplish my goal."

The look on this young man face showed he was scared, worried about failure. But, it also showed me that he had the guts and the courage to try. Think about it; is this possible?

Standing there looking at him, I was thinking to myself, "This young man has heard through the grapevine here at this company that I have helped a lot of people accomplish their goals and accomplished their promotions so he has a little heads up on what to do and what not to do."

As I stood there, I tilted my head, raised my eyebrows, and stared at him with a hard, direct facial expression.

"Do you know what misery loves company means?" I asked.

"Well, sir, I am not sure. If you do not mind, I would like to hear your definition."

I was impressed because this showed that he was thinking before he answers the question. As a compliment, I responded that I was impressed at his answer to the question.

The look on his face just glowed. "Thank you, Sir," he said again.

"One definition to misery loves company is that there are a lot of people: coworkers, friends and family who do not want you to succeed simply because they have not succeeded," I explained.

"They have not, and may not try to succeed. Therefore, they will do and say anything to you to get you to give up and fail. Do you fully understand what I have just said?"

"Yes,sir," he said, his beaming facial expression was priceless. So I asked him if he was a leader or a follower. I could see his facial expression and watch his eyes moving. I knew he was given these questions some detailed thought. I notice that he corrected his body posture, showing pride in his physical appearance. At first, he was standing slouched, and here he was standing at attention.

Then he answered my question. "I am a self-leader, sir."

"OK are you going to be open minded and want to learn what I teach?"

"Yes, sir".

"Are you going to follow what your coworkers tell you to do?"

"No, sir, because I have over heard what they have been telling you."

I explained, "The whole point is misery loves company. They will do anything and everything to tear you down so you do not succeed," I explained.

His eyes shifted from side to side.

"You think about that and we will pick up tomorrow," I said. "That is if you want to do."

"Yes, Sir! I want to definitely pick up where we left off tomorrow, say at 9 o'clock, Sir."

We shook hands and parted.

The next day as I walk to the location of the tool room, I could see that the young man in the room looked very nervous while his coworkers looked occupied.

As I walked up, I noticed very fallow looks that the others were given the young man.

I told the young man I need to talk to him outside of the tool room.

"I see you're having a little problem with the other guys," I said.

The young man looked around at his coworkers to see them frown with disgust. He took a big swallow and said, "Yes, sir."

He spoke up, "I need to tell you I do not have much time before the interview."

"How much time do you have?" I asked.

"One week, sir."

I gave this some thought, and finally said, "Well, young man, this is going to be a cram course. So, are you ready?"

There was a scared look in his eyes, and he started to possibly complain or procrastinate. But, before he could continue to speak, with a very stern voice, but a smile on my face, I asked if he was ready to get to work.

Very firmly, with a stern voice showing confidence and a look in his eyes that impressed me, he said he was.

"All you need are a pen and a notebook," I told him.

"Yes, sir, I have one right here, sir."

"Write this down: Number 1 get that rake out of your hair. Number 2: If you are going to wear a cap like that one you're wearing now that you are wearing sideways, wear it correctly, or don't wear it at all! Number 3: wear some nice shoes, not those untied, dirty, tennis shoes that you are wearing now. Number 4: wear some nice pants, not the baggy ones that you are wearing now that are hanging half off your butt! Number 5: wear a nice shirt, tuck in your pants, and wear a nice belt.

The look on his face was possibly "Oh my God!" because, remember now, both of us are working in a factory plant.

"If you come to work dressed like I have described, then we will proceed with the classes," I said.

He started to say something.

I said, "STOP!" followed with a smile. He stood there and just looked at me as his eyes shifted from one side to the other. What was he thinking to himself? Probably, "Is this guy out of his mind? Or, is he trying to teach me something I don't know?"

I just stood there staring at him. Then, I raised my eyebrows and smiled and asked him "game or not?"

"Yes, Sir, I will do it, Sir!"

The next day, WOW, did this young man get a lot of looks as he walked through the plant to his workstation!

You bet he did, because he was dressed for success, as I suggested. You should have seen the looks I got because I had been helping this young man achieve his goals. At 9 o'clock, we met again, and boy was I impressed!

"Good morning, sir!" he said. I could see in his facial expression that he felt uncomfortable.

"I must say I am impressed," I told him.

I could see a look of relief on his face as he thanked me.

"Now, since time is short, the workload will be doubled, so do not get alarmed," I said.

I asked if he was ready, and he took a deep breath.

"Are you a self-leader? Or, are you a follower?" I asked.

He replied, "I am a leader, sir."

"OK, tomorrow you are going to come into work wearing a tie with your very nice clothes. While you are in the tool room, while you walk, you will practice balancing the book that is in your back pocket on the top of your head. Then when you get home, this is your homework, I want it handwritten so I can read it. Look up the word 'emotion' and write the definition. Then, write a paragraph about how you need to think and speak emotionally.

"Look up the word 'logic' and write down the definition, then write a paragraph about when you think and speak logic.

"Here are 10 quotes from that book, and write a paper on what you think they mean. You are to write three definitions for each quote. Also, write a paragraph on how and when you would use these explanations in applying them to any situation. This will expand your creative thinking.

"Look up the word 'character'. You have six traits of good character pillars: number one is trustworthiness; two respect; three, responsibility; four, fairness; five, earning; six, citizenship; seven, trait keys of success.

Then, number 1, grit; number 2, curiosity; number 3, self-control; number 4, social intellect; number 5, zest; number 6, optimist; number 7, gratitude, moral firmness, self-control, integrity.

"It takes character to endure calamity, so now ask the question, "What is your definition of character, and how do you see it? How do you think it affects your life? Does it have a major or minor impact on others? Does your character have any positive or negative effects towards you wanting to accomplish promotions or goals you want to achieve?"

"Have this done by Monday," I concluded.

"Yes, sir," he replied.

Now, remember this is all taking place inside of a company that is operating like a factory. During the last part of the week, I overheard a lot of gossip about the young man, some good and a lot of criticism. On Friday, we were supposed to meet at 9 o'clock.

As a supervisor, I was headed towards the tool room when I was approached by a co-supervisor. He told me that my supervisor wants to talk to me at 9 o'clock in his office. I asked why and got a gut feeling that someone was trying to put a wrench in the gears, or just shut the whole plan down with my "student".

So I told the supervisor, while looking very stern, that I would be there as soon as I could. I wondered if this was a possible deterrent to my progress of working towards the achievement of the young man who worked in the tool room.

I proceeded to the tool room, and the young man was waiting, dressed in very nice clothes, wearing a tie.

"Good morning," he said.

"Well, good morning to you. Look, we do not have much time. First of all, we are going to act out your job interview. This is what you call a rehearsal, so let's get started."

We both noticed that several coworkers had gathered around, and were watching us. I told the young man to just pretend all of these people were not really there because it would cause a distraction he did not need at this time.

"You must think pure logic, and focus on the rehearsal, understand?" I asked him.

The look on his face, followed by "Yes, sir" while he stood looking at me. "Get rid of that slouched look! Hands by your sides! Head up, chin out, stand on two feet, chest out! Now, I'm going to act like the person who is considering hiring you. I'm going to hard on you and rude. So tell me why you think I should hire you for the position of an assistant manager at my restaurant."

We worked on this for about 30 minutes, while I was pointing out things he may want to change or do differently.

I was amazed at how many coworkers were watching us as we worked.

I proceeded to ask him if, at 10 years of age, his parents told him to go over to the couch and sit there for an hour and keep his mouth shut.

"Sir, I would go and sit down on the couch for an hour and keep my mouth shut, Sir."

"We can all say we all went through this in life. Now, go go back in time and look at the past when you were in school you were led to believe that the teachers and politicians were your imaginary parents and that you felt like you were still a little kid of 10.

"Now, how old are you?"

"I am 23 years old, sir."

"A you going to act as a 10 year-old little boy as you go through life? Or, are you going to act as a fine young man of 23?"

With a stern and a proud voice, and look on his face, he said, "I am going to act my age, sir."

"I compliment you on passing the course with very high scores! Congratulations! I said. But, I still need your homework to be turned in."

The standing audience of coworkers gave us a round of applause, and later, coworkers would thank me for helping the young man who worked in the tool room.

The also thanked me for helping them. I was surprised and asked how I had helped them. They would say things like this with gratitude, "You helped me see that I need to start standing on my own two feet and acting my age."

"I have found that this has paid off in my life to act more professional and now I am seeing the rewards. Thank you."

All of the other workers who were standing around began to clap and I received a huge round of applause!

Then, because the supervisor wanted to talk to me, I proceed to his office. When I arrived, he looked rather disgusted because I was late meeting with him. Or, maybe it was because I did not follow along, treating him as an imaginary parent.

He asked me why I was late. My reply was this, "Sir, you have told all of the supervisors in the supervisors meeting that when we are working on an important matter, we are to stay with it until we see it finished. So, I followed what you have told me in the past, sir."

The look in his eyes could have been that of disgust. He asked why I had disregarded his request to meet with him at 9 o'clock.

"You continued to help the young man who works in the tool room, didn't you?"

"Yes, sir, I believe I have done what you have told us to do. I have completed the matter at hand."

He had no further comments, but he sure said a lot of words with his eyes.

In time, this issue was addressed in the supervisors meeting. I had already been scolded for not following orders, but remember this is not the military. I remember that too that I was giving credit for helping a young man move forward in life.

Actually, I was helping quite a few people accomplish their goals by using my teaching method.

I was scorned by the company because they were one employee short, or probably several employees short.

The following Monday morning, while walking to my department at 7 a.m., I was surprised to see the young man, my student, waiting for me.

He was very well dressed, with his homework in his hand.

"Good morning, sir," he said.

"And, good morning to you, sir," I replied.

"Here's my homework. I would like to say thank you, sir, for all your help."

"You're welcome," I said. He asked if he could share a brotherly hug with me.

The look on his face was sincere, and he had moisture collecting in his eyes.

We shared a brotherly hug followed by a handshake and he stepped back.

"Thank you, sir. I will never forget you, sir. Goodbye."

He turned and walked away. I was standing there watching this young man walk away.

I read his homework and was very impressed with it, so I figured later on that day I would go and visit him at the tool room.

But, when I got there, I noticed coworkers waving their hands at me, and smiling.

I smiled and waved back.

It was nice to see everyone in good spirits at the workplace, but then I thought that this did not always happening on a Monday, maybe Friday, payday, but this was Monday.

So, I proceeded to walk over to the tool room to visit the young man to let him know that he did a great job on his homework and that I was impressed.

But, I got to the tool room only to find that he was not there. I asked his coworkers where the young man was and there was total silence from them.

I asked again and the look on the faces of these coworkers was a combination of happiness and disgust. Then, one of the coworkers said he called in to say he would no longer be working here because he got the job as an assistant manager at a fast food restaurant!

I stood there like all the rest, speechless, thinking on one hand that logically I had helped a young man and his family move forward in life to receive and appreciate the rewards of prosperity, but on the other hand, I am going to miss this bright, eager self-motivated very kind and generous young man. In all, 14 co-workers asked me to help them, and all 14 achieved their promotions!

As a parent, is this something you would like to experience or have?

Parents can work as a team player if they do the exercises, learn the skills, enjoy the humor and prosperity, and pass this on to their kids and relatives.

As a team player, parents have to interact with their children and relatives.

They can actually be doing this every day, because when we talk to them, we grow an emotional bond that will strengthen beyond their wildest dreams!

Logically, the care respect and admiration kids and relatives will have is beyond anyone's wildest dreams, and adults will be amazed. Logically these adults will help them build a very secure, a very stable, and a very solid foundation to deal with all of their issues in life successfully.

Adults need to remember when they were children.

They need to ask themselves: who was the most special relative you always wanted to spend time with? As parents watch their children, they need to think about his favorite relative.

Kids are attracted to those people because they show adults and children the utmost positive motivation, and they send an incentive to them, along with suggestions to enhance the child to think for him or herself with absolutely no negative criticism.

Before you finish this book, I want to tell you that you need to realize that you are not too good to turn down help when it is offered, or when you are asking for help or an opinion.

Do not pretend that you know everything. I've been there. I've done it.

I've been around the world once and sailed the seven seas twice. When asking for help or an opinion, pay attention to every detail because there is probably something to be revealed that will help clear your pathway towards success. When you read this information, and practice the exercise on emotion versus logic, you will notice that this will have a very positive impact on your character.

When you do the exercise on definitions of quotes, you will find that it will have a very positive impact on your character.

When you do the exercise on character, you will be able to reconstruct your character in the utmost, positive way. You will achieve so much good as you live the very best life you possibly can.

Now, start reading this book again and pick up what you missed the first time.

And, make sure you do this with your children.

"Boy!" Why do people get so emotionally upset over the smallest of words or events?

Has this ever happened to you?

Well, it DID happen to me.

Here is my story:

While dating a wonderful young woman in high school, I was invited over to her parent's house for the weekend.

There we would gather for socializing and I was looking forward to visiting with her mother who was a great cook, and her father, a man of great character.

That Saturday, her father was called in to work. So, while we waited for him to return home at the end of the day, there was a very little to do. Because the mother was doing such a good job as a chaperone, I decided to wash my car.

To be polite, and use my manners, I asked her if it would be alright to use their water hose so I could wash and wax my car.

She told me I could, but wanted me to roll up the water hose and turn it off as soon as I finished.

I agreed to do that, and she added that she wanted me to be finished by 4 p.m. so that her husband could park his car in the driveway when he returned home.

They had a small, one car driveway, she explained. For a while, we sat and watched the television show, "All In the Family". I was happy that the television was on, since it gave me something to occupy my time.

Then, I went out to wash my car. As you well know, putting the hose away is the last thing a person does after washing a car.

For some odd reason, my girl's mother thought differently. I was using the spray nozzle, that way I could lay the hose down when I needed to wash.

I was using the chamois to dry the car, but I had planned to use the sprayer to wash my tires and then chamois the hubcaps.

Before I was finished, the woman came out of the house and went over and began rolling up the hose.

"Ma'am, I am not through yet," I said politely. "I still need to wash my tires and hubcaps. Like we agreed, I will roll up the hose when I am finished."

Then, something unbelievable happened.

She reminded me that I had agreed to roll up the hose.

No matter how politely I spoke, explaining I had not completed the job, she became more agitated.

I let her roll it up while I continued to polish my car.

She finally went back in the house, and I was able to unroll it again, so I could finish the job. But, here she came again, barreling out of the house ranting at me.

I tried to explain my actions by saying, "As I told you before, I wanted to wash my tires and hubcaps. I agreed I would roll up the hose when I finished."

She snapped back, "Well, you need to move your car so my husband can park his car in this spot. When he get here, I will tell him you unrolled the hose after I put it away."

There I stood, trying very hard to bite my tongue, stay polite and continue to be well mannered.

Thinking I was supposed to stay the night, and my girlfriend and I were going to sleep on a pallet on the living room floor.

But, that was later. Now, at 4 p.m., my girl's father pulled into the driveway. When he came into the house, me, my girl, and her mother were all watching television.

I actually felt sorry for the father because he had just finished a hard day of work and as soon as he stepped into the house, his wife was already complaining about me.

She complained about my not rolling up the hose after she had rolled it up. I tried to explain, since I looked like the bad guy. "Sir, I was not totally finished before she turned the water off and rolled up the hose," I tried to explain.

He looked at me and rolled his eyes. "I am going to take a shower," he said. "When I get finished, we will eat dinner and watch my favorite TV show."

Later, while we were eating dinner, I could feel the tension and see the body language and different sounds that the wife was using as signals to her husband. She was not pleased with how he was handling her issues and was upset with her husband.

During the show, the wife continued to send body language signals to him.

She suddenly decided that the room was too hot and said she was going to put on something lighter.

She got up, went to the bathroom and came back wearing a negligee with a housecoat with no sash and walked right in front of a fan and the housecoat blew away from her body so that the husband could see more than just the thin material.

He looked at her and stood up to relieve the tension that occurred in his leg area. She looked at him and said, "I think there are some things that are not taken care of, I will just go to bed." She looked at him and her eyebrows dropped down.

"If this is not taken care of, then, I will just go to bed," she said, covering herself.

He looked at me with concern. If he could have talked with his eyes, his message was clear. He was going to watch the rest of the show and head to bed.

"I hope you understand what I am about to tell you," he said. Then, he proceeded to jump down my throat about the water hose. Meanwhile, his wife was fanning the housecoat, revealing more of her negligee. I tried to stand my ground, but, with a stern voice, he said, "Boy, this is my house and my rules! Now, sit down and be quiet, or don't let the door hit you in the ass on the way out of my house!"

I stood there for a few seconds thinking "this is a Catch 22."

First, he is treating me like a 10-year old telling me to sit on the couch and keep my mouth shut. I tried to pretend he was my parent. I took this as a major insult, and second, he was calling me, of all people, "boy".

This made me so furious that I could not believe how or why my blood pressure went through the roof.

I did my best to think logically. I sat trying to control myself and not get emotionally upset. I soon realized the emotion was winning because I was fuming.

As I watched both parents, I saw that they were very happy, maybe even laughing silently.

I stood up and said, "Ma'am, I want to say two things to you: First, that was a great dinner, and second, your wardrobe enhances your physical beauty ma'am." I turned to her husband. "Sir, thank you for the use of your water hose to wash my car. I realized that I have some chores at home I need to do. So, I will be leaving the best of company."

I turned and looked at my girlfriend and saw a great deal of disappointment in her eyes, which were clouded with tears; we would not be sleeping together, that night.

I again expressed my thanks and told them all goodnight as I left their home.

Here was the big issue: I was fuming and my blood pressure was going through the roof because I was being treated as a 10-year old boy, and had been called "boy".

This just ate my lunch as it crawled under my skin. As I drove home, I worked on calming myself down. I figured that I needed to put together a plan to figure out the answers I was searching for.

To explain the extreme effects of what bring emotional upset can do to you one is to lose self-control.

I needed to find a way to control the unexpected emotional feelings that were activated by the smallest of words or issues.

Because if I didn't, there will be a time or times when I would be out of control. This would cause me to say or do something that I would always regret for the rest of my life, maybe something I could never undo.

I finally got home and decided to get a good night's sleep, then start fresh in the morning. I had spent the time traveling home creating a plan.

I went to bed, woke up to a wonderful Saturday morning and was ready to go!

One of the first things I did was get out my dictionary and look up the word "boy". I read the definition, but that only created more questions. I figure I would give this a rest, so I went outside to get something out of my car and noticed my neighbor, Mr. Smith, out in his front yard working in his flowerbed.

I decided he would have likely had many life experiences and could answer my questions. I walked over to his house and his wife came outside and wished me a good morning.

Although I had come to speak to Mr. Smith, I was happy that both of their warm bright cheerful smiles were looking at me as they waited for me to speak.

I told them both that I had stumbled upon an unusual issue and would like to ask their opinions so I would know how to handle it in my life.

I told them I did not want an answer that day, but that they take time to think about it before they tell me their thoughts. I told them I had a riddle-and they both looked at me in a puzzling way.

They asked to hear my riddle.

At first, I felt uncomfortable talking about what had happened to me in front of Mrs. Smith, but she could see that I was embarrassed.

She said I should just pretend that whatever had happened was no big deal. "Just make sure you tell us all the DETAILS because every detail has a major effect on the outcome of an event," she explained.

So, I proceeded to tell them what had happened in great detail. By the time I was finished, the look on their faces showed their surprise.

I noticed that Mrs. Smith did blush, and Mr. Smith had a very big grin on his face as he looked at his wife. He said, "Well, James, that is some experience you went through. We will think about what you told us and get back to you in a few days." I thanked them both.

Mrs. Smith got in touch with me the next day. I admire her for her explanation of the mother of my girlfriend.

She pointed out many things, including one major detail about human nature that helped me understand a great deal.

At this point, I was very happy with myself and gaining a better understanding of the issue. I decided I was also going to ask someone else. I wrote down all of my questions in outline style. I needed to pick one of my high school teachers, ask the same questions, and get their input.

On Monday morning, I tried to decide which teacher would be the best to talk to about my unusual experience. I decided to ask if they would share their thoughts, and my thinking.

As the day went by, I thought about all of my teachers and finally decided on my FFA teacher, deciding I would ask him the next day, before class started.

The following morning, I approached him and asked if I could talk to him after class. He asked if something was bothering me. "Do you have a problem you would like to discuss?"

I responded, "Sir, my problem is a situation where I am trying to find a solution. That is why I would like to meet with you and get your opinion."

I asked if he would be willing to hear my questions and think about them, then let me know his thoughts. I asked him to take the questions home and look them over.

I told him that when we met to talk, he could give me a logical explanation. I noticed, as we talked, that his eyebrows went up and his eyes widened and sparkled.

His smile went from "are you kidding" to a serious, happy expression.

He said, "Well, James, you seem to have this well thought out. Did you write all of your questions down?"

I relied, "Yes, sir, I did," and handed him the paper where I had written all of the questions, as well as some of the background information.

"I hope I can give you some direction on the path of life you are on," he said.

I thanked him, happy and excited, eager to hear his thoughts. But, I did not hear from him for days.

I began to think he had forgotten about me, but tried to keep an open mind.

However, the following Monday morning, the FFA teacher asked me to stop in his office after school.

As the day went on, I tried to concentrate on my other classes. But, it was difficult because of the suspense of what the FFA teacher would be telling me.

Finally, the day ended, and I was excited as I went to his office. When I saw him, he had an unusual smile on his face. "Hello, James, please sit down," he said.

In his tone of voice, I was wondering if I was in trouble. But, then he began to speak. "James, I have given this a lot of thought and even talked to other adults about this. Most everyone came to the same conclusion; so don't get offended by what I am about to say."

I just sat there with a blank look on my face, staring at the teacher, trying to think in a purely logical way.

"Sir, just say what you have to say. I realize the world is not a bed of roses. I asked for your help. I thank you and admire you for going to the extreme to include others to help you reach whatever decision you made.

"I am not perfect and make mistakes in life, but I am trying to learn from my mistakes, as well as try not to make any stupid mistakes," I said.

"I have put together this plan to try to learn how to observe all issues carefully, before I respond to them. I also want to learn a better understanding of two words I don't know the definition of. For example, how do you know the answer to a question if you don't know what the question is?"

I continued on, "During the conversation, I was trying to hold my emotions and that is very difficult because observing your facial expressions, I can clearly see the emotion in your eyes."

We both paused for a moment and I could see a bit of moisture in his eyes. We both took a deep breath and I continued to look at his serious facial expression.

"Sir, I am asking you to say whatever you have to say. I am a young man and I am a big boy, so I can appreciate whatever you have to say."

I watched him and saw the expression on his face relax. "OK, I see that you are ready, then let's get started," he said.

He put his hand on his chin, and took a second look at me. "James, in society, I don't know when a boy turns into a young man. I do know people much older than myself. When they don't get their way, they act like a child; they definitely do not act their age," he said.

"That brings me to your situation. But, first I am going to ask you some questions."

I agreed to answer them.

"James, how old are you?" he asked. "Sir, I am 15," I responded.

"Do you live with your parents?"

"Yes, sir, I do."

"People like your girlfriend's father, who is much older than you, have experienced more things in their lives than you have. You have not gained these experiences. Therefore, they can't see themselves from back when they were your age."

He went on to tell me, "They remember the dumbest boyish things they did. Now, you are doing the same things they were doing at your age. That is why people much older will call you "boy".

"Yes, you are entering the stage of a young man. Enjoy being 15 years old, and about to enter the young man state of your life. Do not try to be someone you are not. Enjoy your age and act your age. Before you know it, you will be my age. I am sitting here looking at you, remembering when I was your age. I remember some of the most childish things I did because I was trying to be someone I was not.

"If I had one wish, it would be that I had done what you are doing right now.

"With the plan you have laid out, I would have had far greater accomplishments in my life, that what they are today.

"I hope I have helped you because you sure have helped me on the road of life." It was my turn to speak, and I asked, "Sir, when I am your age can I still be a boy at heart?"

He smiled and said, "I don't see why not."

Most people are spending their time trying to tell everyone else how to live their lives. You are on a good road and you are spending time productively, and that is the best way to live your life."

I responded, "Thank you, sir."

We shook hands and what had just happened created a bond between us. From that day forward, my life changed. My girlfriend's mother, father and I all achieved a silver lining in our relationship.

I received compliments from my high school teachers and many others. Even today, I am told people appreciate and admire about my attitude and character.

Get an idea, develop a plan to do your homework. Do your research, get a second and third opinion and compare your options for your future.

You can get upset, or go on the defense because you are assuming the definition of the words.

Logically, you can take time to do the research so you will be fully aware of what the word means in your life.

Now that you have read this book, go back and do the three exercises together with your family.

Review the past, add it to the present, and reap the rewards the future has in store for you.

Are You Concerned?

There are so many people who are concerned about their family's educations. Why?

Students who graduated from high school before 1977 were encouraged to go to college, while having a GPA equivalent of a sophomore.

Around 1977, politicians passed a Bill that lowered the National Grade Point Average (GPA). These scores were so low that the students couldn't pass the college entrance tests.

In 2021, our children were locked out of their schools due to the COVID pandemic.

Here are some troubling statistics that not only affect our children, but the future of this country!

* The United States is falling behind the rest of the WORLD
* The economy of this country is affecting the education of all students in the United States!
* What we perceive is totally different than reality.

If we want to take back what we once had, and have a much higher quality of living and economic stability, teach not only children, but adults what this book says!

Learn these methods and not only will each of our lives improve, but so will our entire country! Learning how to be motivated and successful and move forward in life are the keys to success!

REMEMBER:

* BE PROUD OF YOURSELF, BE HAPPY, BE PROUD OF WHO YOU ARE AND YOUR BACKGROUND AND LEARN SELF-CONFIDENCE.
* NO ONE CAN TAKE THE BEST FROM YOU!
* DON'T GET EMOTIONALLY UPSET. LEARN HOW TO LOOK AT THINGS FROM A WHOLE NEW WAY, BOTH AT WORK AND AT HOME!

"Big Secret"

has three effective methods

to lead people to achieving their goals

in LIFE!"

-James Markham, Author

JWMARKHAM3@gmail.com